THE EUCHARIST AS A
COUNTERCULTURAL LITURGY

THE EUCHARIST as a COUNTERCULTURAL LITURGY

An Examination of the Theologies
of Henri de Lubac, John Zizioulas, and Miroslav Volf

Yik-Pui Au

Forewords by
Pan-Chiu Lai and Luther E. Smith, Jr.

PICKWICK Publications · Eugene, Oregon

THE EUCHARIST AS A COUNTERCULTURAL LITURGY
An Examination of the Theologies of Henri de Lubac,
John Zizioulas, and Miroslav Volf

Pickwick Publications
An Imprint of Wipf and Stock Publishers
199 W. 8th Ave., Suite 3
Eugene, OR 97401

www.wipfandstock.com

PAPERBACK ISBN: 978-1-4982-7930-7
HARDCOVER ISBN: 978-1-4982-7932-1
EBOOK ISBN: 978-1-4982-7931-4

Cataloguing-in-Publication data:

Names: Au, Yik-Pui | Lai, Pan-Chiu, foreword. | Smith, Luther E., Jr., 1947–, foreword.

Title: The eucharist as a countercultural liturgy : an examination of the theologies of Henri de Lubac, John Zizioulas, and Miroslav Volf / Yik-Pui Au ; forewords by Pan-Chiu Lai and Luther E. Smith, Jr.

Description: Eugene, OR : Pickwick Publications, 2017 | Includes bibliographical references and index.

Identifiers: ISBN 978-1-4982-7930-7 (paperback) | ISBN 978-1-4982-7932-1 (hardcover) | ISBN 978-1-4982-7931-4 (ebook)

Subjects: LCSH: Lord's Supper. | Liturgics. | Christianity and Culture. | De Lucbac, Henri, 1896–1911. | Zizioulas, John, 1931–. | Volf, Miroslav, 1956–.

Classification: BV601.5 .A93 2017 (paperback) | BV601.5 .A93 (ebook)

Manufactured in the U.S.A.   04/04/17

In memory of my parents, Sum and Wai-Lan,
and my beloved pastor James E. Nichols

Contents

Foreword by Pan-Chiu Lai

How Christian faith is to be related to the public issues is an important question for contemporary Christian churches. For Christians living in a secular and/or religiously pluralistic culture, how to respond to the seemingly dominate "non-Christian" culture is a particularly urgent challenge. In order to respond to this kind of challenge or problem, many Christians endeavor to address the relevant issues through biblical studies, systematic theology, and Christian ethics, etc. Some interdisciplinary dialogue between Christian theology and social sciences are also involved. In these endeavors the relevance of the study of Christian liturgy is often overlooked. Part of the reason for this neglect may have to do with the assumption that the Christian worship is supposed to be conducted within the church's four walls and solely for the religious needs of the faithful. It is thus irrelevant to the Christian practice in the public sphere. However, it is noteworthy that as the famous motto *lex orandi, lex credendi, lex vivendi* indicates, the way of Christian living should follow the way of their believing, and the way of their believing the way of their worship. According to this understanding, how Christians should live in public square should be eventually shaped by their worship. It is then a crucial task to explore whether and how the Christian worship may inform Christians the way of practicing their faith in their daily livings, including their livings in the public sphere.

The present book is evolved from the doctoral thesis of Yik-Pui Au, an experienced church pastor participating proactively in the public life in Hong Kong. It consists of an innovative attempt to explore the countercultural function of the Eucharist through examining the theologies of John Zizioulas, Henri de Lubac, and Miroslav Volf, who represent the Catholic, Orthodox and Protestant traditions respectively. Instead of offering an "exegetical" study or systematic articulation of their theologies *per se*, this book creatively and courageously integrates some of the theories and research findings from three different disciplines, namely, ritual theory, history of Christianity, and theology of culture, in order to articulate a heuristic framework to analyze the cases of these three theologians.

The analyses are focused on the relationships among their theological interpretations of the Eucharist, the cultural issues or problems they identified, and whether and how these two poles are linked up. After analyzing these three cases individually, a comparative evaluation of the three cases is included. Both the analysis and evaluation concern mainly whether and how their interpretations of the Eucharist address validly and effectively the cultural issues they identified —namely hierarchical culture in the case of de Lubac, individualism in the case of Zizioulas, and social exclusion in the case of Volf. Needless to say, the explorations of the three cases can be more comprehensive and there are some other cases deserving to be studied. This innovative and experimental study, including the interdisciplinary heuristic framework developed for the analysis of eucharistic theologies, is to be highly appreciated.

This book may contribute to not only the ecumenical dialogue among the theological traditions within Christianity, but also the Christian churches' awareness of the relationship between liturgy and culture. Its potential contributions to the recent discussion concerning the integration between ecclesiology with ethnography should be further explored. I wholeheartedly recommend this book to professional theologians, church workers and lay persons who care about the relationship between Christianity and contemporary culture.

Pan-Chiu Lai
Associate Dean (Research)
Professor, Department of Cultural & Religious Studies
The Chinese University of Hong Kong
May 30, 2016

Foreword by Luther E. Smith, Jr.

READING *THE EUCHARIST AS a Countercultural Liturgy* expands my understanding and experience of the Eucharist as a transformational sacrament. I believe it is a seminal contribution to eucharistic literature and ritual studies.

Dr. Yik-Pui Au focuses on culture as the lens for perceiving the purpose of the Eucharist and the conclusions of its theological interpreters. The Eucharist is a sacrament to transform culture. Going deep into the meanings of the Eucharist requires one to appreciate God's passion for the world. And cultural realities influence the theologians who interpret the Eucharist's meanings. Culture is both a subject for transformation by the Eucharist and a force that informs understandings of the Eucharist.

When Dr. Au argues that the Eucharist is countercultural, she explains that her use of the countercultural concept does not imply negating the value and necessity of culture. She recognizes that culture is a complex reality with many diverse expressions—some nurture and liberate while others destroy and oppress. The Eucharist liturgy is a countercultural ritual act when it challenges those cultural expressions that fail to conform to God's dream for creation.

The Eucharist liturgy also challenges the church to enact the Eucharist with the awareness of its transformational purposes for culture and the church. Too often the church embodies cultural values of domination and injustice. The church must be vigilant in assuring that the Eucharist liturgy is opening hearts and minds to God's creative work in the world.

Contentious debates occur among Christian churches about the Eucharist liturgy. What is the meaning of the Eucharistic elements? Who is authorized to consecrate and serve the Eucharistic elements? Who is invited to the Eucharist Table? The answers to these questions are so central to core beliefs of ecclesial identities that often Christian ecumenism has been stymied because of differing convictions regarding the practice of the Eucharist. Such contentiousness begs the question: "Is the Eucharist a uniting or divisive sacrament for Christian churches that work toward fulfilling Jesus' prayer "that they may all be one"?

This book does not attempt to address all the issues about the Eucharist and its practice. It offers a more fundamental insight: the Eucharist is a Christian ritual that asserts Christian identity and commitment for a more just and neighbor-loving world. Fulfilling this purpose involves transforming culture. And as essential, it involves transforming church communities that harbor unjust, domineering, and alienating behaviors in their internal life and social witness.

Dr. Au's engagement of Henri de Lubac, John Zizioulas, and Miroslav Volf is a stimulating analysis of insights about the Eucharist from these three major theologians. These theologians' perspectives reveal how intense Christian devotion and rigorous scholarship do not result in a common understanding of the sacrament. At the end of the most intellectually faithful efforts to interpret the Eucharist, multiple faithful interpretations remain. Such multifarious outcomes are a sign of a ritual's power to generate meanings that are never exhausted by one tradition. The truest response to explicating a ritual is not about coming to a definitive conclusion. The truest response is appreciating that a ritual's meaning needs to be continually pursued. I believe that ongoing efforts to embrace a faithful understanding of the Eucharist will benefit from being in conversation with this book's insistence on the liturgy's countercultural purpose.

Luther E. Smith, Jr., Ph.D.
Professor Emeritus of Church and Community
Candler School of Theology, Emory University
April 6, 2016

Preface and Acknowledgments

EVER SINCE THE EUCHARIST was instilled by Jesus Christ in the upper house, the sacrament *par excellence* has been celebrated by churches regardless of denominational or theological differences, albeit their ways to partake in it vary. Despite such variation, one thing remains unchanged in the Eucharist. It signifies and sustains the Christian identity of ecclesial communities in the midst of cultures which contradict Christian mission and values. A careful survey of early church history reveals that the egalitarian sharing in early ecclesial meals began as witnesses against the prevailing social stratification culture in Greco-Roman society. Put in contemporary terms, the Eucharist started as a countercultural liturgy. Yet this function of the Liturgy was watered down by the Christian church becoming the state religion of the Roman Empire since the fourth century. In medieval times, the heated debate on eucharistic realism further undermined this function of the Eucharist. The countercultural voice of the Eucharist was dimmed, if not muted. Not until the second half of the twentieth-century, there was resurgence of interests in discussing the transforming function of the Eucharist regarding culture.

Recent scholarship in this area has offered multiple interpretations of the Eucharist and its relationship with culture. The diversity in interpretations is understandable and expected in light of the rich power of this ritual. Still what is needed is a cross-church tradition research to highlight the differences and commonalities among various denominations regarding the relationship between the Eucharist and culture. This approach is significant not just for academic pursuit, but also for ecumenical effort to resist cultural trends contradictory to Christian value by drawing upon the most ancient repertoire of Christianity, the Eucharist.

In this book, I attempt to fill the research gap. I want to explicit the countercultural function of the Eucharist against some prevailing cultures, namely, individualism, social exclusion, ecological exploitation, and hierar-chal cultural trend by adopting a cross-church tradition approach. Henri de Lubac, John Zizioulas, and Miroslav Volf, whose theologies of the Eucharist are studied in this research, represent the Catholic Church, Orthodox Church, and Protestant Church respectively. They are included because of their insightful interpretations of the Eucharist and also its relationship to culture. Through this book I hope to contribute to the scholarship on the Eucharist, the liturgy *par excellence*, for the purpose of reinforcing the Christian identity in the midst of tides of different cultures.

This work is an extension of my PhD dissertation. I would like to take this opportunity to thank those who helped me in my PhD program journey and in the course of writing. A very special word of gratitude for supervision is owed to Prof. Pan-Chiu Lai, my PhD advisor, for his effective supervision as well as prompt and constructive responses to my questions and search for guidance. Like other students, I have been delighted by his subtle humor in class and also chats outside of classes. He has just the right blend of scholarly spirit and sense of humor. I would like to thank Prof. Luther E. Smith, my supervisor while I studied at Emory University. His opinion of my academic aspirations played a major part in my decision to pursue a PhD. I appreciate Dr. Kin-Ming Au and his wife Dr. Wai-Man Yuen for their advice for my academic pursuits. I wish to thank Prof. Peter C. Phan and Prof. Anselm K. Min for giving valuable comments on this work. To Rev. James E. Nichols and his wife Lois, I cannot thank them enough for their prayers and love. I wish to thank my great friends, Dr. Samuel Kent and his wife Lydia who are always generous in both spirit and countenance to me. Their faith in my ability to finish the program was encouraging. I really appreciate my fellow student Miss Wai-Hang Kung whose company I enjoyed very much through the PhD program. It was very kind of her to help fix the formatting of the first manuscript for me. Of course, any errors that remain are entirely my responsibility. I am indeed grateful to another fellow student Miss Sze-Ting Lam for her caring words and acts of kindness showered upon me when she learned that my mother died rather unexpectedly. At that time my dissertation still had three more chapters to finish. Her kindness lightened my sadness and helped me recollect myself to resume writing after my mother passed. I am immensely thankful to my dear sisters Yuen-Yee and Yik-Choi for their love and support which go beyond words.

I would like to thank Mrs. Lynn Poling for patiently and professionally proofreading my manuscript and giving useful comments and corrections. I would also like to thank the editors of *The International Journal of Orthodox Theology* and *Sino-Christian Studies: An International Journal of Bible, Theology & Philosophy* for permitting me to use part of the papers I published in them. I wish to thank the staff at Pickwick in Oregon for their professional help in making my dissertation into a monograph. Any deficiencies in this book are mine.

Finally, this book is dedicated in memory of my parents, Sum and Wai-Lan, and my beloved pastor James E. Nichols.

Yik-Pui Au
The Chinese University of Hong Kong
June 22, 2016

1

Introduction

As the sacrament *par excellence*, the Eucharist occupies a prominent position in Christianity because it is celebrated by all Christian churches through all ages. There has been an enormous increase in attention to the Eucharist from biblical narratives of the early Christian celebrations to the thriving scholarship of contemporary liturgies. In addition, the Eucharist is also an important issue in ecumenical dialogue. For example, one of the evidences of this ecumenical concern was captured in *Ways of Worship* issued in 1951 by the Faith and the Order of the World Council of Churches (WCC). In a concerted effort, the ecumenical family members shared the scholarship of their liturgical traditions. This joint effort did not just reflect the enormous attention paid to the existing worship traditions, but also ways in which the experiments in "liturgical creation" made possible.[1] One of the fruits of such a co-operative endeavor was the acknowledgment of the need of liturgical renewal or reform, especially in the eucharistic *ordo* and the eucharistic prayer.[2] The heightened academic and ecclesiastical attention given to the Eucharist in *Ways of Worship* exemplified the blossoming development of the liturgical and ecumenical movements in the twentieth century. Ecclesial communities of different traditions came to re-recognize the significance of the Eucharist in Christianity.

However, is the importance of the Eucharist confined to the church as a religious practice or ecumenical conversation? If it is accepted that the

1. Edwall et al., eds, *Ways of Worship*, 15–16.
2. Spinks, *Remembrance*, 378.

1

church should be a witness or even a herald of God's Kingdom to come to the temporal world, would the Eucharist, as the liturgy *par excellence* of the church, have something significant to convey to the world? In particular, can it be related to the concrete societal or cultural needs of the wider society? If the answer is negative, it becomes necessary to explain why the most significant sacrament of the church is irrelevant to society, in contrast to the church's self-understanding that she is important to human society. If the answer is positive, then it is essential to examine in what ways it may influence society.

It is necessary to find answers to these questions. On one hand, research has been done on the inculturation of liturgy which focuses on liturgical reformation in order to make it fit into diverse cultural contexts. On the other hand, there have been some studies on the Eucharist and culture highlighting a perspective that the Eucharist embodies alternative social visions that are different from the prevailing culture. For example, Hal Taussig explains research on the holy meals in the early church thus:

> These meals need to be conceived as spiritual experiments as well. By this is not meant that they were occasions for mystification of real-life issues, retreat from social realities or intellectual quests, or some kind of prototype for later Christian liturgy. Rather, the meals enacted the new social alternatives so vividly that the meal participants experienced themselves as actually a part of a new social order.[3]

Put differently, the "new social alternatives" enacted by the Eucharist in the early church can be different or contrary to the prevailing cultural currents of the contemporary society.

Partly inspired by the studies on early Christian meals, this book will explore whether and how the Eucharist can function to enact visions of new social orders that are different from the mainstream. The term "countercultural" is employed in this study to denote this function. In this book, the term countercultural is not the same as "against culture,"[4] as explained by H. Richard Niebuhr in *Christ and Culture*; countercultural here means neither a total rejection of the value of culture nor an affirmation of the necessary contradiction between Christianity and culture as a whole. It does not refer to establishing a sub-culture that is diametrically opposed to and isolated from the cultural mainstream or *ethos* of a particular society.

3. Taussig, *Meal*, 54.
4. Niebuhr, *Christ and Culture*, 48.

Rather, the definition of countercultural in this research means upholding the identity and values of the Christian community against the cultural
currents of the contemporary society because of the new social alternatives
embraced by the Christian faith. Countercultural here also means resisting
some particular cultural trends, particularly those embodying the values
and/or worldviews contradictory to those of Christianity. In a broad sense,
the church's proclamation, liturgy, and other embodiments of Christian
values or worldview can be countercultural as well, albeit their countercultural functions are not noticed by the communicants. However, the church
can also make use of, for instance, its liturgy, to deliberately counter certain
cultural trends within the church or in the larger society. In particular, this
book focuses on the assertion of Christian identity by the Eucharist, the
liturgy *par excellence*, which may resist the influences of those cultural currents on particular Christian communities or even in the wider society as
a whole.

As such, the Eucharist can be intended as countercultural. This book
is based on this narrower sense of the word countercultural. The theological
tasks related to this kind of countercultural liturgy may involve: identifying
the cultural trends to be countered, stipulating the countercultural implications of the Christian liturgy, and exploring how the church may counter
certain cultural trends effectively through the administration, interpretation, and even renewal of the Christian liturgy.

Furthermore, the theological discussion of the countercultural liturgy
does not exclude the possibility or intention that the countercultural liturgy, as a strategy, may eventually contribute to the goal of transforming
the culture of a particular society. In this sense, borrowing Niebuhr's typology, those Christian theologians who engaged in the discussion concerning
countercultural liturgy may be more congruent with the "Christ the Transformer of Culture" type,[5] and therefore are not necessarily to be classified
as representatives of the "Christ against Culture" type.

Besides defining the term countercultural, it is important to point out
that this study is conducted on the assumption that the church is a cultural
minority within the larger society. This assumption is supported by Stephen B. Bevans's observation that in the twenty-first century, churches find
themselves the minority in more and more non-Christian as well as multicultural societies. As the minority in a multi-cultural and multi-religious
world, churches are compelled to assert the uniqueness and difference

5. Ibid., 190.

of Christian faith.[6] Therefore, the alleged countercultural function of the Eucharist is a way to insist that Christian identity should receive further attention. Moreover, this assumption of church as the minority in society is congruent with the historical studies of early Christians. The early Christian communities were the minority in the Greco-Roman society and their communal meals were in fact countercultural. Further descriptions and explanations of early Christian meals can help support the validity of this assumption in this book.

The early Christian meals were social practices forming the identity and way of life of the faithful who were the minority against the Roman imperial power as well as the Greco-Roman cultural milieu. Like Hellenistic meals, which were the loci of social activities, communal meals were the center of activities of the early Christian communities. Taussig has thoroughly researched the early Christian meals in the first century. Against the canvas of the Hellenistic communal meal etiquette, he underscores the countercultural behaviors in those meals against the oppressive Roman regime and also the stratifying cultural currents of the Greco-Roman world.[7] For example, in Hellenistic meal protocols a reclining posture, which was generally reserved for free citizens, actually reinforced social stratification. The reclining order actually embodied the social code.[8] However, in the early Christian meals, socially marginalized people reclined together with the community. This meal practice could be envisioned as a social experiment different from or even subversive to the stratifying culture of the time. The placing of marginalized folks reclining at the table together challenged the "honor shame code" of Hellenistic culture.[9] Furthermore, this social experiment actually educated the participants to relate to each other in anticipation that they would behave differently towards one another. Moreover, the libation after the *deipnon* associated with Jesus' blood and the new covenant in early Christian meals pledged the participants' allegiance to and anticipation of the Kingdom of God.[10] This libation constituted a countercultural act by the early Christians toward the Hellenistic culture

---

6. Bevans and Williams, *Contextual Theology*, 5–6.

7. Taussig, "Festive Meals," 21–54.

8. Smith and Taussig, *Many Tables*, 33–34.

9. Taussig, *Meal*, 150.

10. Klinghardt, "Communal Meal," 10. In Greco-Roman world, meals were consisted of two parts. The first one was *deipnon* the serving of food. It was followed by libation leading to *symposion*, which involved drinking party, entertainment, and discussions.

of raising the cup to the emperor or other gods. During the *symposion*, songs sung in the early Christian meals were cosmic, signifying the cosmic significance of Jesus' crucifixion. Such singing created intense tension between the power of the Roman regime and the anticipation of the Kingdom to come.[11] The libation and the singing in the early Christian meals embodied the countercultural gestures against the hierarchical and totalitarian cultural currents of the Roman Empire. These countercultural behaviors happened in semi-public settings where strangers might have dropped in uninvited, or the outside world could peep through the large window of the dinning place to see what was happening in Christian meals.[12] Though there may be variations in detailed practices from one meal community to another, the early Christians were actually displaying their countercultural nuances or behaviors consciously through their meal practices to proclaim their awareness of the mainstream culture that challenged their Christian identity and values. They reinforced the self-understanding that they, as Christian meal groups, were meant to be countercultural.

Although the first century Christian meals were not as formal expressions of the Eucharist as contemporary Christians might imagine,[13] these early Christian meals, which exemplified countercultural tenor, evolved into a more uniform liturgy of the Eucharist as the church developed.[14] Paul Bradshaw explains this growing uniformity in that as the church became more developed, liturgical variety usually decreased. Furthermore, after the Peace of Constantine, the church's desire for the liturgy to remain countercultural was supplanted by the desperate need to deal with the pagans who were flooding into the church. According to Bradshaw, the demarcation between pagan and Christian started to blur in the fourth century.[15]

The abovementioned historical account of the countercultural tenor of the early Christian meals in the first century lends support to this research into the Eucharist as a countercultural liturgy. In recent decades there has been re-kindled interest in the liturgy of the Eucharist and also eucharistic ecclesiology in different Christian traditions. However, there is a lack of comparative study of how the Eucharist can counter cultural currents in different church traditions. Therefore, this research investigates

11. Taussig, *Meal*, 135.

12. Ibid., 102.

13. Ibid., 156.

14. Smith, *Symposium*, 4–5.

15. Bradshaw, *Origins of Christian Worship*, 64–65.

the interpretations of the Eucharist by Henri de Lubac, John Zizioulas and Miroslav Volf, who represent the Catholic, the Orthodox, and the Protestant traditions respectively, and examines whether and how their theologies can counter the cultural currents within their own contexts. In chapter 2, recent and relevant scholarship in the following three areas is reviewed to lay out the basic research landscape: the relationship between liturgy and culture, theology and culture, and theology and liturgy. It also captures the research niche of a cross-church tradition study of the Eucharist and justifies choosing the approaches of de Lubac, Zizioulas, and Volf for this research project. It is significant to highlight that this book is not just a cross-church tradition study of the Eucharist but also an interdisciplinary study of theology, culture, and ritual. Thus for methodology, three approaches are used to bring the Eucharist as a countercultural liturgy to the foreground: the theology of culture, the religious studies, and the historical approach. It also delineates a four-step method to analyze how these three theologians correlate the Eucharist to cultural currents identified by them. The four-step method includes: (1) analyzing the theologian's theological interpretation of the Eucharist; (2) identifying the cultural currents addressed by the theologian; (3) examining how the theologian counters cultural currents by the Eucharist; and (4) evaluating the countercultural function of the theologian's interpretation of the Eucharist. In chapters 3, 4, and 5, the theologies of the Eucharist of de Lubac, Zizioulas and Volf, and how their interpretations of the Eucharist can help counter the cultural currents identified by them are examined respectively by using this four-step method. Chapter 6 takes a comparative approach to evaluate these theologians' eucharistic theology with the aim of assessing their interpretations of the Eucharist as a countercultural liturgy. The comparative evaluation will be organized around four areas: (1) awareness of cultural currents; (2) diagnosis of cultural currents; (3) correlation of the interpretations of the Eucharist to cultural currents; and (4) effectiveness in countering cultural currents. The framework of trinitarian participation is employed as a common plane for comparative assessment of the correlation of the interpretation of the Eucharist to cultural currents. The three theologians' understanding of the trinitarian participation in the metaphysical, soteriological and ecclesiological aspects of the Eucharist is then evaluated. Chapter 7 draws conclusion concerning the significant findings of this research. In addition, an overall evaluation of any common limitation of their interpretations of the Eucharist is addressed. An assessment is also made regarding what aspect and to what extent these three theologians may complement each other. In other words, would there be anything in their interpretations of the Eucharist that would help buttress each other's approach? Furthermore, a critique is made of how well each represents his own ecclesiastical traditions and to what degree each one's limitations are exemplified within those traditions.

In sum, this research is undertaken on the basis that the Eucharist can be studied as a countercultural liturgy. It tests how this claim can be substantiated by the three theologians' interpretations of the Eucharist according to their own church traditions and how they argue that the Eucharist can counter the cultural currents in a particular society. It is hoped that this research can contribute to the revision of the conventional understanding of the Eucharist, which is rather confined to salvation and the church. Last but not least, it is also hoped that this research can exemplify the possibility of conducting an interdisciplinary study of a specific aspect of the Eucharist across different church traditions and bring the complexity and rich texture of the multifaceted interpretation of the Eucharist to the foreground to invite further research in this direction.

2

Recent Studies and Methods

LITURGICAL, CULTURAL, AND THEOLOGICAL STUDIES ON THE EUCHARIST

SINCE THIS BOOK INVOLVES a study of liturgy, theology and culture, it is necessary to first review recent and relevant scholarship on the relationships between liturgy and culture, theology and culture, and theology and liturgy in order to investigate the basic background of this research. This review is to show that there is a research niche of an interdisciplinary study on the countercultural function of the Eucharist by using a cross-tradition approach.

Liturgy and Culture

Subsequent to the close of the Second Vatican Council (1965), the liturgical reforms ratified by *Sacrosanctum Concilium* (The Constitution on the Sacred Liturgy) have been a driving force behind the phenomenal growth of research in this area. Catherine Vincie crystallizes the historical development of liturgy reforms after the Council and differentiates the major approaches to reform liturgy, namely classicist, adaptation, and inculturation.[1] Margaret Mary Kelleher regards the purpose of inculturation as

---

1. Vincie, *Celebrating Divine Mystery*, 170–71.

concretizing the church in a diversity of local and cultural contexts around the world.[2] While she endorses the liturgical inculturation as one of the aspects of the broader project of inculturation of the church, she goes further, asserting that inculturation should also include mutual critiques of the parties involved.[3] Anscar J. Chupungco goes beyond the parties being involved in the liturgy for the purpose of inculturation. He advocates that for liturgy to be inculturated, it must also be contextualized in such a way as to be prophetic to the cultural current. He stresses that the contextualization of liturgy is in line with Christianity's prophetic role.[4] By drawing upon the prophetic tradition from the Old Testament, Nicholas Wolterstorff also underscores liturgy as prophetic, because it is not for the atonement of sin but rather for criticizing sin.[5] He regards liturgy as criticism against cultural values and practices that dissuade people from striving after God. Yet, Wolterstorff is quiescent about how the dynamics of liturgy can be a source for people to live a life congruent with the values found in liturgy.

Keith F. Pecklers focuses on the modes of worship liturgy to culture stipulated in the "The Nairobi Statement on Worship and Culture": transcultural, contextual, counter-cultural, and cross-cultural.[6] He believes that the ability to employ these modes determines the credibility and future of the church.[7] Pecklers is emphatic about counterculture, recalling the wane of counterculture in worship of the church in the Middle Ages and its revival under the legacy of Martin Luther.[8] The faithful have to take note that there are times when it is necessary for the church and it's liturgy to be countercultural. Terico Bretanha Junker's dissertation "The Prophetic Dimension of Liturgy: Transformative Liturgy Seeking Social-economic Justice" is an attempt in this direction. He recognizes celebration of liturgy as fertile soil for learning and teaching so as to transform human consciousness toward socio-economic justice.[9] This preponderance of evidence shows that there

---

2. Kellenher, "Liturgy, Culture," 108.

3. Ibid., 109.

4. Chupungco, *Liturgical Inculturation*, 21.

5. Wolterstorff, "Authentic Liturgy," 14–15, 17.

6. Pecklers, *Worship*, 133. The Statement was penned at the Lutheran World Federation Conference in Nairobi, Kenya in 1996.

7. Ibid.

8. Ibid., 168–69.

9. Junker, "Prophetic Dimension of Liturgy," 2.

is an emerging thought that liturgy not only can be, but should be counter-cultural; it forms the theoretical basis of this research.

Theology and culture

Since this book is also an interdisciplinary study of the relationship among liturgy, culture, and theology, the connection between theology and culture naturally has to be examined. The book *Changing Conversations: Religious Reflection and Cultural Analysis* offers discourses on concerns of culture, politics and economics from the perspectives of both religion and culture.[10] The inter-connected relationship between theology and cultural studies and way of living has received attention in *Converging on Culture: Theologians in Dialogue with Cultural Analysis and Criticism.*[11] Kathryn Tanner offers a thorough account of the integration of theology and cultural studies. She emphasizes the operation and opportunity of theology with respect to everyday cultural practices, and also cultural negotiation.[12] Graham Ward asserts that theology is continuously involved in cultural negotiation.[13] The relation between Christian discourses and cultural transformation is apologetic (social representation of theology), evangelical (Christian mission), and doxological (advancement of the Kingdom).[14]

Like Tanner, Kelton Cobb also considers everyday cultural practices in perspective. He identifies and discusses theological themes embedded in everyday cultural activities like movies, TV programs and music. In a Tillichian perspective, Cobb claims that there is always a reality that cannot be reduced to power and social conflict.[15] In close connection to power and social conflicts, cultural studies is particularly interested in power relations conveyed in all kinds of cultural expressions; in some ways theologians share this interest. Gerald A. Arbuckle is intrigued by how cultural studies can furnish social issues for theological reflections on church life and mission. He examines the findings of cultural studies in power, social exclusion, and identity negotiation and analyses their impacts on both the

10. Hopkins and Davaney, *Changing Conversations*, 2.

11. Brown et al., eds., *Converging on Culture*, v–vi.

12. Tanner, *Theories of Culture*, 85.

13. Ward, *Cultural Transformation*, 4.

14. Ibid., 8–9.

15. Cobb, *Theology and Popular Culture*, 100.

process and substance of inculturation.[16] In *Furthering Humanity: A Theology of Culture*, T. J. Gorringe adopts liberation theology to inquire into power issues and reflects on how the church relates to power in a multicultural world.[17] Pan-chiu Lai, in "Cultural Studies and Theology in Tillichian Perspective," suggests that besides handling power issues in cultural representations in terms of sin, theologians have to offer theological responses to alienation unveiled by cultural studies. A reinterpretation and explanation of Christian symbols is needed in order to conquer alienation carried out in cultural representations in everyday life.[18]

Among the scholarships of Christian symbols, Tillich's influence cannot be overlooked. His idea of the transcendent and the immanent level of symbolism enriches the understanding between symbol and people's everyday lives. The transcendent level of symbolism is not in empirical reality and the immanent level of symbolism happens in concrete culture.[19] Tillich emphasizes overcoming the gap between transcendence and immanence by the sacramental.[20] Immediately, he uses the materials in the Eucharist to illustrate the symbolism.[21] He focuses on the sacramental in the relation of culture to everyday life and emphasizes the immanent religious symbolism. Regarding everyday culture, Lieven Boeve perceives the sacrament as a reflection of sacramental life and thought, and its expression in people's daily lives. He deems the living out of such reflection and expression in accordance with the open, non-hegemonic Jesus narrative in daily life important.[22] As such, sacramental living bears witness against "hegemonic narratives,"[23] which are basically induced by exclusion of others. Louis-Marie Chauvet further concretizes sacramental presence (way of living) by focusing on eucharistic presence. The breaking of bread is the very figure of the eucharistic presence of Christ, namely, *kenosis*, which should be produced in the faithful as an ecclesial way of life.[24] This idea has significant

---

16. Arbuckle, *Culture, Inculturation, Theologian*.

17. Gorringe, "Liberation Theology and Cultural Politics," 149–73.

18. Lai, "Cultural Studies and Theology," 79.

19. Tillich, *Theology of Culture*, 61.

20. Ibid., 64.

21. Ibid.

22. See Boeve, "Sacramental Presence," 22.

23. Ibid., 16.

24. See Chauvet, "Broken Bread," 261.

implications for the concern of this research: the liturgy of the Eucharist can form the faithful to counter cultural currents.

Theology and Liturgy (Especially the Eucharist)

The above review has shown that liturgy can be regarded as countercultural; therefore, as a natural extension, the Eucharist can be studied as a countercultural liturgy as well. Since there has been a resurgence of interest in eucharistic ecclesiology in the second half of the twentieth century, further review of the relation between theology and the Eucharist can help update the readers regarding development in this area. Presently there are publications on the Eucharist that bring different theologians or traditions together in a comparative approach. For instance, Paul McPartlan's *The Eucharist Makes the Church* compares John Zizioulas and Henri de Lubac's eucharistic ecclesiology.[25] Stephen Bentley Sours brings the voices of Thomas Aquinas and John Wesley together in his dissertation "Eucharist and Anthropology: Seeking Convergence on Eucharistic Sacrifice between Catholics and Methodists."[26] Richard A. Nicholas employs a comparative study method to focus on Thomas Aquinas's thought on the Eucharist with respect to the theological and philosophical thought of Donald Keefe.[27] Some scholars opt to study the phenomenological aspect of the Eucharist. For example, Nathan Halloran's "The Flesh of the Church: De Lubac, Marion, and the Site of the Phenomenality of Givenness."[28] Donald L. Wallenfang studies how the notion of "givenness" of Husserl, Heidegger, and Marion, who are philosophers of phenomenology, contribute to the interpretation of the Eucharist.[29] Taking a more historical approach, Lee Palmer Wandel revisits the different understandings of the Eucharist and the consequences in the Lutheran, Reformed and Catholic traditions of the sixteenth century, in *The Eucharist in the Reformation: Incarnation and Liturgy*.[30] In field study, Janine Paden Morgan's dissertation "Emerging Eucharist: Formative Ritualizing in British Emerging Churches" compares

---

25. McPartlan, *Eucharist Makes the Church.*

26. Sours, "Eucharist and Anthropology."

27. Nicholas, *Eucharist as Center*, 1–2.

28. Halloran, "Flesh of Church," 29–44.

29. Wallenfang, "Sacramental Givenness," 131–54.

30. Wandel, *Eucharist in Reformation.*

and gives dynamic reflections on the Eucharist of different churches with the spiritual formation in sight.[31]

The above review demonstrates one major research gap: there is not yet any research on theology and the Eucharist across different church traditions that puts the cultural significance of this liturgy into perspective. Since the Eucharist is a liturgy *par excellence* and also a focal point of ecumenical dialogue, this research will examine the theology of the Eucharist of Henri de Lubac (1896–1991), John Zizioulas (1931–), and Miroslav Volf (1956–), representing the Catholic, Orthodox and Protestant traditions respectively. The choice of these three theologians is based on the following reasons. De Lubac was renowned for his re-interpretation of ecclesial meaning of the Eucharist through scrupulous historical study, and he was a pioneer in constructing eucharistic theology, making the Eucharist the cornerstone of his theology. De Lubac's theology also countered the individualistic, totalitarian and hierarchical trends of contemporary culture. Zizioulas is well acknowledged in the Orthodox tradition. His extensive writings on the Eucharist and eucharistic ecclesiology have received profound attention from ecumenical circles. He identifies the individualistic culture and the exploitive culture on environment. He explains how the Eucharist helps address these cultural tendencies. As a Protestant theologian who has proposed an egalitarian ecclesiology for the Free Church, Volf's theology may be relatively less eucharistic in comparison with de Lubac and Zizioulas. Yet, Volf is well aware of the countercultural function of theology and he is the founding Director of the Yale Center for Faith and Culture. This credential reflects his interests and experiences in investigating relations between faiths and cultures. Furthermore, he did a comparative study on Zizioulas and Joseph Ratzinger, which will make the comparison with Catholic and Orthodox approaches more probable. In addition, he is novel in adopting the ancient traditions of the Eucharist in his theological writings to address the cultural current of social exclusion. It is hoped that a comparative study that draws upon the respective traditions of these three theologians will shed light on their interpretations of the Eucharist that will highlight the countercultural functions of this liturgy. The following section will stipulate the research method to conduct this comparative study.

31. Morgan, "Emerging Eucharist."

METHODOLOGY

Before delineating the approach of this research, it is necessary to examine methods or theories that help establish grounds of the first part of this thesis, "The Eucharist as a Counterculture Liturgy." First, in order to support how this research may contribute to the recent theological scholarship, some recent studies that use the theology of culture approach in order to focus on the cultural meaning of the Eucharist will be reviewed. Second, the general theory of ritual in religious studies will be examined to illuminate the countercultural function of liturgy. Third, some historical studies, which illustrate that the early Christian liturgy was countercultural, will be re-visited. Finally, the method of research in the second part of this thesis is explained: an examination of the theologies of Lubac, Zizioulas, and Volf will be stated for investigating whether and how they may counter the contemporary cultural currents based on their interpretations of the Eucharist.

Theology of Culture Approach

While the traditional theological approaches focus on either ontological questions of transubstantiation and consubstantiation, or ecclesiastical questions about its relationship to the church, there is a new approach focusing on the cultural significance of the Eucharist. Some scholars have researched the countercultural function of Christian liturgy. For example, H. Paul Santmire claims that liturgy can function as a "community-forming ritual" in the contemporary culture for pursuing peace, justice, and also ecological hope. He applies the theory of liturgy as countercultural to shaping ecclesial communities in order to address ecological crisis.[32] Margaret Scott makes use of the eucharistic texts to counter a host of cultural currents like poverty and disparity, and how the eucharistic texts can be a "counter-narrative" by remembering Jesus' ministry to the poor and outcaste.[33] Gordon W. Lathrop adopts the countercultural dimension of liturgy to re-envision how baptism and the Eucharist may re-map political and ecological ethics against exclusivism and earth-abuse.[34]

James K. A. Smith's approach is the most explicit with regard to the methodological issues. The methodology of this research is quite similar

32. Santmire, *Ritualizing Nature*, 35–36.

33. Scott, *Eucharist and Social Justice*, viii.

34. Lathrop, "Eucharist and Earth-Care," 125–52.

14

to James Smith's liturgical anthropology in his books *Desiring the Kingdom* and *Imaging the Kingdom*. Therefore, a review of James Smith's approach is useful to this research. He stipulates that liturgy can be pedagogy of counterculture. He bases this theory on a liturgical anthropology that sees humans as embodied actors, whose identities and desires are not just shaped cognitively but also unconsciously through liturgy. Christian worship can be an "alternative cultural formation."[35] There are four key elements in this model.[36]

First, human beings' fundamental way of attending the world is through love or desire. James Smith argues from the point of a robust "Augustinian anthropology,"[37] which advocates that human beings' identities and their primary orientation to the world are defined by what they love. He criticizes the rationalist pedagogy based on a worldview that has been predominant in the intellectual circle as inadequate in inscribing such an orientation. He argues that humans are dynamically intentional when they take aim at the world as an object; they are not merely intellectual storage boxes of static ideas or beliefs.[38] What they love shapes their intentionality towards what they care about. Their ultimate love is what they worship.

Second, this love or desire aims at some vision of a good life. Our ultimate love moves and prompts us because we are more enticed by some vision of a good life at the precognitive level than by propositional ideas at an intellectual level. Our hearts and pursuits are captivated not by cognitive ideas, but by a picture of what a flourishing life should look like. This vision of a good life is inculcated into us by narratives, myths, images and icons. When these can capture our imagination of a good life, our hearts rather than our minds are engaged to strive for such visions. For example, James Smith uses the image of "the kingdom" to refer to the vision of the good life that people would like to pursue, though he further qualifies that different people may have different visions of what the Kingdom should look like.[39] Most importantly, what James Smith argues here is that human beings are motivated pre-cognitively, rather than at an intellectual level.

Third, our love or desire intended for the world is formed by a set of habits. Our desire for and intentionality toward a particular vision of

35. Smith, *Desiring Kingdom*, 35.

36. Ibid., 46–62.

37. Ibid., 46.

38. Ibid., 47–48.

39. Ibid., 54.

a good life moves and motivates us when it becomes an integral part of our habits. James Smith argues that because human beings are predominantly desirous and imaginative animals, their desire for the Kingdom is impressed on them through their habits and functions, which are basically unconscious.[40] They walk in the world as actors with habits imbued into them, and they react to the surroundings without consciousness. This precognitive dynamic is not inborn but woven into us by a long development of habits.

Fourth, the habits are formed in us through affective and physical means. In particular, the physical practices such as routines, ritual, and liturgy are closely connected to our bodily senses. James Smith further elaborates that the bodily involvement in ritual is formative in shaping habits through repeated practices that converge our hearts toward certain ends. As liturgical animals, we have our love primed by liturgy that grasps our hearts to aim at certain ends, that is, the Kingdom of God.[41]

In *Imaging the Kingdom*, James Smith also draws upon Maurice Merleau-Ponty, Pierre Bourdieu, and Mark Johnson to support the thesis that liturgy can be countercultural. He adopts Merleau-Ponty's theory of preconscious knowledge that our physical response to the world is primarily precognitive or preconscious.[42] James Smith interprets preconscious knowledge as our habitual way of being in the world.[43] Our body can acquire habits unconsciously and our habitual body can render a way of life that is our culture. He further explains how Christian liturgy can form the habitual body to live a way of life counter-culturally by turning to Bourdieu's *habitus*.[44] *Habitus* is a set of structured and structuring dispositions imbued into our body by past history. *Habitus* is "structured" structure that comes to us from outside and has conditioned the constitution of our world. It is also "structuring" because it moves us to constitute the world in some particular way.[45] *Habitus* is inside the body, which can be formed through rituals. James Smith also emphasizes that a social body can co-opt and incorporate a body into it by rituals. He further uses Johnson's concepts of metaphor and narrative to illustrate how these help our body to

40. Ibid., 56.
41. Ibid., 40.
42. Merleau-Ponty, *Phenomenology*, 94.
43. Smith, *Imagining Kingdom*, 44.
44. Bourdieu, "Structures," 52–65.
45. Smith, *Imaging Kingdom*, 81.

organize meaning aesthetically.[46] In sum, liturgy can prime our imagination and response to the outside world through metaphors and narratives, and very importantly, bodily involvement in ritual routines. James Smith also stresses that by immersing bodies in a liturgical environment, human beings can be imbued with a metaphorical inclination toward the world.[47]

Both of James Smith's books, *Desiring the Kingdom* and *Imaging the Kingdom*, explain that the physical involvement in liturgy can shape and direct the participants to have a disposition toward a particular end, that is, the Kingdom of God. James Smith's studies support that the shaping and forming of one's inclination toward some sort of human flourishing takes more than discourses, which intellectually communicate worldviews. While there are some scholars, for example Martin D. Stringer, who focuses on Christian worship as discourse in which Christian language changes in order to reflect the changing Christian worldviews in history,[48] James Smith argues that bodily involvement in liturgy is significant for forming disposition. Being imbued by liturgy, the participants are helped to counter certain cultural currents in their ordinary lives. This argument supports the thesis that the Eucharist as a liturgy can induce the participants to counter cultural currents in a particular social context that may be contrary to Christian identity and values.

Religious Studies Approach—General Theory of Ritual

The general theory of ritual also supports the method of this research in that liturgy can be studied as countercultural.[49] The dictum of Jonathan Z. Smith—"ritual is, above all, an assertion of *difference* (emphasis added)"[50]— succinctly explains that ritual is contrasted with ordinary activities to show

---

46. Johnson, *Meaning of Body*, 209.

47. Smith, *Imaging Kingdom*, 124.

48. Stringer, *Christian Worship*, 14–23.

49. Some theorists argue that ritual sanctions existing social order rather than counter cultural currents. For example, Emile Durkheim explains how the negative rite (ways to prohibit certain ways of acting by the faithful) and the positive rite (the acts that draw the faithful closer to the sacred) work together to maintain the status quo of a totemic clan. Durkheim, *Elementary Forms*, 303–4, 330. However, historical studies on early Christian church reveal that the empirical experience of early Christians with the Eucharist did exemplify the countercultural function of the Liturgy.

50. Smith, *To Take Place*, 109.

"what ought to have been done was not."[51] He states that the function of the contrast between ritual and the counterparts in ordinary activities is to assert difference and arouse attention. In other words, ritual is a deliberate contrast between everyday life and the place of ritual; ritual can run contrary to the culture.

Furthermore, Catherine Bell's idea of ritualization and ritualized body explains how liturgy can cause cultural formation. She explains:

> Ritualization is a way to generate privileged contrasts between the acts being performed and those being contrasted or mimed so as to produce ritualized bodies—actors imbued with the dispositions to engender practices structured by such privileged contrasts— which are perceived in turn to promote the restructuring of the larger cultural milieu.[52]

According to Bell, ritualization is a process in which the construction of ritual environment and activities impress upon the ritualized body schemes of the way things ought to be.[53] Through ritualization, the ritualized body internalizes those schemes as principles, appropriates other cultural situations, and generates "strategic schemes" to the world outside the ritual to counter certain cultural currents.[54] For example, the act of early Christians who took the initiative to take left over bread to the poor, who were oppressed by the military emperor, was a nuanced response to counter the cultural current of inequality in society. According to Bell's ritual theory, therefore, liturgy as a rite can prime the body to react differently to the predominant culture outside the churches.

Historical Approach—Re-visiting Early Christian Liturgy

The approach of this research is further supported by some significant studies of early Christian liturgy. Some recent studies show that liturgy was practiced to shape the early Christian community as countercultural.[55] In particular, Paul F. Bradshaw critically assesses a host of ancient church

---

51. Ibid.

52. Bell, "Ritual Body," 304–05.

53. Bell, *Ritual Theory*, 98–99.

54. Ibid.

55. For example, Attridge, *Apostolic Tradition*; Bradshaw, *Early Christian Worship*; *Eucharistic Origins*; Dix, *Shape of Liturgy*.

documents on church order and life.[56] They contain descriptions and instructions for baptism, the Eucharist, ordination, and other rites developed in early church history. He finds that in early Christianity (up to the fourth century) the self-understanding of Christians was to set themselves over against the world and avoid adopting liturgical practices that appeared like those of other religions, which may cause the Christian faith to become lax.[57]

Taussig suggests ritual analysis as a new method for studying the early Christian meals. He gives a critical review on major ritual theorists and how their theories can complement or challenge each other in the study of Hellenistic meals.[58] He also highlights the similarities and differences between Hellenistic meals and early Christian meals. His studies reveal how the early Christian communities reflected that they were a counter-society to Rome through their meal rituals.[59] Besides, the association of the early Christian meals with the cross shaped the Christian identity, which was to be lived outside the meals. Taussig highlights that the meals of the early Christians were social experimentation against the status quo in Greco-Roman society; that is, gender and ethnic tensions.[60]

In addition to Taussig's works on the countercultural experimentation in the early Christian meal, Gordon W. Lathrop explains that Christian liturgy is orientational in the sense that it has an ethical meaning borne by liturgy that is to be acted out in our lives.[61] Wayne A. Meeks also proposes the idea that a morality distinctive from the surrounding cultures, which is shaped by Christian liturgy, is the key that makes the early Christian communities countercultural.[62] He asserts that Christian liturgy provides a structure that gives a guide of moral reasoning and a framework of interpretation between ritual and common life experience.[63] Therefore, liturgy is not only about doing things but also telling things or making sense through

---

56. Bradshaw, "Ancient Church Orders," 80–110. In this chapter, Bradshaw reviews the origins, contents, and contexts of various ancient documents on church orders. He also tries to establish the chronological and literary relationships between them.

57. Bradshaw, *Search for Origins*, 65.

58. Taussig, "Ritual Analysis," 55–66.

59. Taussig, *Meal*, 109–11.

60. Ibid, 158–59, 163–64.

61. Lathrop, "Cardinal Directions," 51.

62. Meeks, *Christian Morality*, 4.

63. Ibid., 97.

doing.[64] For example, Santmire argues that the early liturgy was not for sanctioning the status quo but was culturally transformative. He cites the mingling of water with the sacramental wine in one single big chalice from which people, regardless of their class, could drink at the Eucharist table,[65] and compares the loving act of giving bread to the poor with the Roman Empire's accustomed celebration of violence through brutal killing.[66] These were not for maintaining or endorsing the status quo; rather they were raising alternative values and behaviors contrary to the predominant culture outside the churches. Lathrop also notes that in the early church, the commensality at the Eucharist table was rather subversive to the exclusive and hierarchical culture in the Hellenistic world.[67] The collection for the poor at the meal and the giving of bread to the needy after the meal were "ripples" into the world outside the Eucharist.[68] In other words, this egalitarian attitude and self-giving love shaped by the Eucharist overflowed into the ordinary world.[69] In a nutshell, these historical studies of early Christian liturgy point to how that liturgy had countered the cultural current in that particular society. The above review of some of the recent interpretations of the cultural dimension of liturgy, general theory of ritual, and the historical studies of early Christian liturgy have converged to support the thesis that liturgy can be countercultural. As a natural extension of this conclusion, the Eucharist as the sacrament *par excellence* can be studied as a countercultural liturgy.

However, it is well to be cautious here. Though the Eucharist can be a countercultural liturgy, Bell cautions that many factors influence the impact of ritualization on a ritualized body and also the world outside the rite. One example is the extent of people's involvement in the ritual, frequency of reiteration, and the degree to which the schemes or values embedded in the ritual are endorsed by the social life outside the ritual.[70] It is worth observing that liturgists can be the worst enemies of liturgy. Perhaps Bell's

64. Ibid., 110.

65. Santmire, *Ritualizing Nature*, 37, 39. The poor people who could not afford to bring wine were welcome to bring water and poured it into the one single big chalice for sharing together.

66. Ibid., 43–44.

67. Smith and Taussig, *Many Tables*, 32–33. Dinning at different tables with different postures and cuisines served was a matter of social stratification.

68. Lathrop, *Holy People*, 195.

69. Meeks, *Christian Morality*, 92.

70. Bell, *Ritual Perspectives*, 252.

caution explains why some scholars would like to conduct ethnography on concrete liturgical life and its impact on ecclesiology.[71] However, David F. Ford reminds us that thoughts and practices are not separated. He raises a question of what sort of thought will help most and asks for a theologically informed anthropological study of eucharistic practices.[72] In a spirit of self-critique, scholars who conduct ethnographical studies on ecclesiology also make specific remarks on the need of theology in their research. Paul S. Fiddes reminds us that a purely inductive approach may lead to "relativism and a floating free from the Christian tradition."[73] In a similar vein, John Swinton believes that theology is indispensable in ethnographical studies on religious communities because theology cannot be bracketed off from the investigation of meanings happening in those religious communities. Moreover, theology helps the reflexivity of the researchers.[74]

Rather than ethnographical studies, which tend to focus on the practice itself, this research will adopt a theological approach and focus on the theological interpretations of the Eucharist. This is not to ignore or deny the importance of ethnographical studies, but to recognize and fill the research gap of the theological account of the Eucharist with respect to cultural currents across the Catholic, Orthodox, and Protestant traditions. It is also hoped that outcomes of the research may help the theological basis of ethnographical studies on the future practice of the Eucharist.

THE METHOD TO EXAMINE THE THEOLOGIES OF DE LUBAC, ZIZIOULAS, AND VOLF

The following method is devised to evaluate how the interpretations of the Eucharist of these three theologians may connect the theological and ecclesiastical meanings of the Eucharist to cultural currents in their respective contexts, whether and how they mull over the countercultural aspect of the liturgy.

First, the theologian's interpretation of the Eucharist is analyzed. The works of each of these three theologians is surveyed and the theological

---

71. Morgan, "Emerging Eucharist"; Veliyannoor, "Transformation." There are also other studies which address the methodology of ethnography and its relation to ecclesiology. For example, Ward, *Perspectives on Ecclesiology*.

72. Ford, *Self and Salvation*, 165.

73. See Fiddes, "Ecclesiology and Ethnography," 19.

74. See Swinton, "'Where is Your Church?'" 83–84.

interpretation of the Eucharist of each theologian is analyzed within his own theological system or construction. The purpose of this step is to posit the role of the Eucharist in one's theology as a whole. The assumption here is that if one's theological interpretation of the Eucharist has a significant role in his theological construction and tradition, the more likely that the relationship between the Eucharist and cultural currents is stronger in his theology and his theological heritage.

Second, the cultural currents addressed by the theologian are identified. The goal of this step is to find out cultural currents that the theologian has attempted to address and how he examines the impact of the cultural currents on society and also the ecclesial community.

Third, how the theologian counters cultural currents by the Eucharist is examined. This step scrutinizes to what extent and depth the counter to the cultural currents identified by the theologian is connected to or based on his interpretation of the Eucharist.

Fourth, the countercultural function of the theologian's interpretation of the Eucharist is evaluated. This step will examine how the theologian interprets the cultural significance of the Eucharist. Then, the validity of his interpretation in the formation of the counterculture will be evaluated. Assessment will be made to see if there are any biases, inadequacies, and questionable presumptions in the interpretation of the Eucharist.

SUMMARY

In this chapter, the survey of literature reveals that there is a research gap in the countercultural function of the Eucharist across different church traditions. The approaches of theology of culture, religious studies, and also historical studies of early Christian liturgies are examined to support how they converge to support that the Eucharist can be envisaged as a countercultural liturgy. Finally, the four-step method is delineated to make an inductive study of the theologies of the Eucharist of, and also the cultural currents identified by de Lubac, Zizioulas, and Volf. Their work is analyzed and evaluated in order to determine whether and to what extent the cultural significance of the Eucharist is integrated into their theologies. The criteria of this analysis are two-fold: how the theologian interprets the cultural significance of the Eucharist and how valid is his interpretation in the formation of counterculture. For de Lubac, it is reasonable to expect that the Eucharist is cardinal to his theological system because his axiom "the Eucharist makes the Church" gives profundity to the eucharistic ecclesiology after him.[75] However, his idea of the Eucharist as a liturgy countering the totalitarian cultural current as well as the hierarchical cultural current must first critique the Catholic Church of his lifetime. As for Zizioulas, he has profound awareness of the relevance of the Eucharist to cultural currents because of his extensive writings on the Eucharist, individualism, and ecological crisis. It is expected that he profusely draws upon his Orthodox tradition to support the cultural significance of the Eucharist regarding countercultural influences. In light of the ecclesiology which Volf has constructed for the Free Church and also his Protestant heritage, Volf may not give as much theological emphasis to the Eucharist as de Lubac and Zizioulas have offered. However, his theology has potential for making connections with cultural currents such as social exclusion. Yet, he may need to draw upon other traditions to complement his interpretation of the Eucharist in order to counter exclusive culture.

75. De Lubac, *Corpus Mysticum*, 88.

3

Henri de Lubac's Interpretation of the Eucharist

Countering the Individualistic, Totalitarian, and Hierarchical Cultural Currents

INTRODUCTION

THIS CHAPTER EXAMINES HOW Henri de Lubac SJ (1896–1991) connects his theological interpretation of the Eucharist to the cultural currents identified by him, namely, the individualistic, totalitarian, and hierarchical cultural currents. Since de Lubac's interpretation of the Eucharist is intrinsically connected to his theology of the church, a summary description of his sacramental or eucharistic ecclesiology is necessary for analyzing and positioning the place of the Eucharist in his theology. Based upon the analysis called for, the cultural trends identified by de Lubac are outlined in order to see whether and how his interpretation of the Eucharist can counter the cultural currents identified by him. Finally, the validity of his countercultural interpretation is assessed.

To begin, it is helpful to point out the background against which de Lubac formulated his theological ideas of the Eucharist. De Lubac adopted the medieval spiritual exegesis as an intellectual framework to interpret the relation between the church and the Eucharist.[1] His emphasis on the inextricable connection between spiritual exegesis, the church, and the Eucharist is supported by the organic connection among them during the Middle Ages. Marie Anne Mayeski astutely pays attention to this intrinsic triad relationship:

> The liturgy was the primary context within which medieval Christians heard, read and understood the Bible. It is not surprising, then, that the liturgical context shaped significantly the process, methods and style of biblical interpretation throughout the Middle Ages. The structure of both the Eucharist and the Liturgy of the Hours impelled the exegete to read the biblical text with certain important presuppositions. The existence of a real worshipping community, often enough known to the interpreter, provided a concrete audience for his exegesis.[2]

To further illustrate this triad relationship, Mayeski explains that from the liturgical structure of the Eucharist, medieval exegetes discovered the principles of typology, which were fundamental to all applied exegesis. Another example is that since the Liturgy of the Word in the Eucharist moved inevitably to performing in the sacrament of thanksgiving ministered, the exegetes of the Middle Ages used this as a model for moving from hearing the word to the obligation of doing it.[3] Furthermore, in medieval times, spiritual exegesis and biblical commentary were usually the arenas in which political, philosophical and theological concerns were discussed.[4] From these examples, de Lubac makes an accurate point when he emphasizes that spiritual exegesis and the Eucharist were intrinsically united in the ecclesial setting in the Middle Ages. The cultural role of spiritual exegesis in medieval times also helps explain de Lubac's use of spiritual exegesis in re-engaging the Catholic theology with contemporary thought or culture.[5] In pursuing this passion, he became a leading figure of the New Theology movement, which was a return to the patristic studies in Scripture, spiritual exegesis, and liturgy in the late 1940s.[6] Given the enormity of de Lubac's *oeuvre*, this chapter is not a comprehensive investigation of all his work.

1. Wood, *Spiritual Exegesis*, 1.
2. See Mayeski, "Reading the Word," 61.
3. Ibid., 62.
4. Spijker, *The Multiple Meaning*, 1.
5. Komonchak, "Theology and Culture," 584.
6. Wood, "Henri de Lubac," 318–20.

Specific attention is given to those writings that are more apparently related to the Eucharist, the church and culture.

DE LUBAC'S INTERPRETATION OF THE EUCHARIST

The Impact of Nature-Supernatural on the Eucharistic Ecclesiology

De Lubac's concept of the connection between the natural and the supernatural lays the ground of his sacramental eucharistic ecclesiology. He consistently fought against the notion of "pure nature," which is separated from the supernatural or grace.[7] He succinctly summarizes this theory of dualistic pure nature that "In the complete system, the two series—pure nature and supernaturalized nature, or nature called to the supernatural—flowed along parallel channels in complete harmony."[8] De Lubac judges that this notion was a misreading of Aquinas's *desiderium naturae* in human beings for God.[9] This misreading has caused the church to adopt a more remote attitude toward the social and cultural situation of the larger society.[10] He argues profusely against pure nature because it is too extrinsic that nature and the supernatural are mutually impermeable.[11] De Lubac adopts Maurice Blondel's explanation that the supernatural is not extrinsic to human beings but an incorporation which ensures "both the union and the distinction of two incommensurables,"[12] without annihilating human nature. De Lubac's understanding of Aquinas makes him re-assert that there is an interaction between nature and the supernatural without demolishing each of them. He further elaborates that Aquinas's idea of nature is to see God as "the desire of his nature,"[13] which indicates the presence of the "beatific vision" to a human being.[14] To substantiate the connection between the divine and nature, de Lubac also highlights the infusion of God's Spirit into

---

7. De Lubac asserts his position against the notion of pure nature in his three publications: *Surnaturel, The Mystery of the Supernatural,* and also *A Brief Catechesis on Nature and Grace.*

8. De Lubac, *Mystery,* 41.

9. Milbank, *Suspended Middle,* 16–17.

10. Komonchak, "Theology and Culture," 584–91.

11. De Lubac, *Brief Catechesis,* 38.

12. Ibid., 48.

13. De Lubac, *Mystery,* 58.

14. Milbank, *Suspended Middle,* 16.

human beings and becomes a "principle of life."[15] More importantly, if there were no interaction between nature and the supernatural, then there was no Incarnation of the Word, which renders the Eucharist an inefficacious symbol. So also for *Epiclesis*, the sign of the Holy Spirit by whom the flesh of Christ is prepared and intervenes in the consecration of the Eucharist for the making of his Mystical Body, also comes to naught.[16]

This interaction between nature and the supernatural is crucial for de Lubac's interpretation of the sacrament. Without this interaction, the sacrament would have failed to be an instrument of grace through which human nature can be united to God. Only because of this correspondence between nature and the supernatural, can the sacrament be mediatory between them. The sacrament signifies the supernatural to humans, who by partaking of the sacrament, is united with the supernatural or the divine. *A fortiori*, the Eucharist, which is the sacrament *par excellence*, mediates between the supernatural and the natural. As such, the Eucharist is mediatory between the supernatural and nature, and forms an important foundation of de Lubac's sacramental eucharistic ecclesiology.

De Lubac's nature-supernatural also has consequences for his ecclesiology concerning the role of the church. David Grumett comments that de Luabc's refutation of pure nature is also prompted partly by a concern for the vanishing of a sense of the sacred.[17] Grumett explains that though de Lubac notes that nature and the supernatural are of different orders and there should not be any blasphemous confusion, one must remember that nature is made for the supernatural. The whole order of human nature and also the destiny of humanity is thus drawn to and shaped by the supernatural. Therefore, the church should not present herself as a mere human society nor should she model herself after any secular order, but should embrace the divine vocation and communicate it.[18]

While de Lubac stresses the natural desire for the supernatural, there are still doubts about his contention. John Milbank questions whether the natural desire *per se* is the working of grace. If it is a natural desire, why is it grace then?[19] Furthermore, if grace is given, there must be a giver and a recipient. Then there ought to be a moment for exchange, of giving and

15. De Lubac, *Brief Catechesis*, 42.

16. De Lubac, *Catholicism*, 62.

17. Grumett, *De Lubac*, 21.

18. De Lubac, *Brief Catechesis*, 109–11.

19. Milbank, *Suspended Middle*, 32.

receiving.[20] However, how is God subject to the temporalization in such an exchange? Nathan Mitchell responds (on behalf of de Lubac) to Milbank thus: first of all, temporalization never subjugates God, who is Creator of time, and second, human beings do not stand before God as recipients for they are the gifts themselves. God's creation of human beings does not result in recipients, because their entirety—their whole life and existence is given *per se*.[21]

One more argument can be directed against Milbank's query. Why must there be some sort of exchange here? Milbank's critique probably assumes the view advocated by some anthropologists or cultural theorists that there is no pure gift and the giver will receive something one way or the other in return.[22] However, de Lubac succinctly answers that the natural desire or longing for the supernatural is a "capacity for divine being born of a *lack* (emphasis original) in the depths of the soul, rather than from the beginnings of a possession."[23] Nevertheless, de Lubac's stress on the interaction between the supernatural and nature forms an important basis of his eucharistic ecclesiology, without which the Eucharist cannot be mediatory.

The Significance of the Unity of the "Three Bodies of Christ" to the Eucharistic Ecclesiology

The unity of the three bodies of Christ, namely, the historical body, the sacramental body and the ecclesial body—forms the crucial foundation of de Lubac's eucharistic ecclesiology.[24] The Eucharist is the sacrament signifying the sacrifice of the historical body of Christ and also the ecclesial body, meaning the church, which will be complete in the *eschaton*. Thus, the Eucharist sacramentally unites the salvation history of the past (memorial), the present (the rite), and the future (*eschaton*).[25] Without the unity of these three bodies of Christ, de Lubac's theology ceases to be eucharistic.

De Lubac proves the significance of this unity by doing a scrupulous historical study of the medieval shifts in the eucharistic language. Since the birth of Christianity, the Eucharist has been inextricably connected to

20. Mitchell, "Contextualizing," 279–80.

21. Ibid.

22. Ibid.

23. Grumett, *De Lubac*, 21.

24. De Lubac, *Corpus Mysticum*, 256.

25. Wood, *Spiritual Exegesis*, 51, 59.

the church. In the early patristic view, there was a unity in the three-fold body: the historical body of Christ born of Mary, his eucharistic body, and his ecclesial body. Until the middle of the twelfth-century the term *corpus mysticum* referred to the Eucharist but not the church.[26] De Lubac traces the history thus: due to the doctrinal change in the Eucharist caused by Berengar of Tours,[27] in which the essence of the bread and wine becoming the body and blood of Christ was feared to be lost, the church reacted by emphasizing the real presence of Christ in the Eucharist by calling the Eucharist *corpus verum* (true body). Since then, the link between the eucharistic body and the body of Christ born of Mary has been reinforced at the expense of the diminishing link between the eucharistic body and the ecclesial body or the church. As a result, eucharistic realism won over ecclesial realism. Later, both the eucharistic body and the ecclesial body lost the word *mysticum*. By the middle of the twelfth century, *corpus mysticum* referred to the church only, without any reference to the Eucharist. De Lubac criticizes this reaction of the church to Berengar because it resulted in the severance between the church and the Eucharist. This is demonstrated by the fact that the real presence dominates the doctrine and the Eucharist has lost its place in the Christian Mystery, its impact on spirituality, and most importantly, the unity of the church.[28]

De Lubac highlights the repercussion of this loss of unity in the three bodies, pointing out that, without any reference to the Eucharist, the church has been reduced to a social body like a mere congregation.[29] The separation of the mystical eucharistic body from the visible church damages both the church and the Eucharist. The reduction of the church to be a visible society without any reference to the Eucharist has caused the loss of the sense of sacred. When the church views itself as an institute more than a sacrament of mystery, over-institutionalization becomes the result of the temptation of self-perpetuation. It also leads to individualistic piety because the sense of mystery and community signified by the Eucharist are no longer associated with the church. Eucharistic piety becomes more an individualistic devotion.[30]

---

26. De Lubac, *Corpus Mysticum*, 248.

27. Wandel, *Eucharist in Reformation*, 19–21; Rubin, *Corpus Christi*, 16–20.

28. De Lubac, *Theology in History*, 229.

29. De Lubac, *Corpus Mysticum*, 249.

30. Ibid., 259.

The Eucharist as a Sacrament of Unity

De Lubac highlights that the Eucharist, as the sacrament *par excellence*, is an instrument of unity through which the union of human beings with Christ is renewed and strengthened in the broadest sense.[31] He states that this union between Christ and human beings is a social matter rather than an individual one. As sacrament, the Eucharist does not establish an individual relation between "the soul and God or Christ."[32] Instead, each individual receives grace as he or she is joined socially to the body of Christ, from which flows the saving power. The Eucharist exists in and for a society, the church, which is the "society of the Spirit.[33] De Lubac, in supporting this point, calls upon a train of names of the Fathers and their relevant writings.[34]

The Eucharist is also the sacrament of unity that embodies Catholicism. According to de Lubac's interpretation, the Eucharist contains unity of all humanity and thus embodies the genuine Catholicism of the spiritual unity into Christ.[35] This genuine Catholicism is the universal unity of humanity in Christ, which is nothing like a "cosmopolitan individualism."[36] Dennis Doyle comments that de Lubac's idea of Catholicism is radically inclusive.[37] In Doyle's analysis, de Lubac intends to alert us to the narrow vision of Catholicism embraced by the church, which is caused by "extrinsicist views of the supernatural."[38] This extrinsicist view accounts for the complacency of the church toward the secular powers. De Lubac connects the Eucharist with Catholicism, which is definitive to his theological career since his mission is to renew Catholicism in order to re-unify the spiritual unity of all humanity and re-engage Catholic theology with culture.

In explaining the source the Eucharist's unity, de Lubac once stated that "The Christian mysticism of unity is trinitarian,"[39] which is the supreme model of unity. However, in most of de Lubac's interpretation of the Eucha-

---

31. De Lubac, *Catholicism*, 48.

32. Ibid.

33. Ibid.

34. Ibid., 52–54.

35. Ibid., 48–63.

36. De Lubac, *Theology in History*, 450.

37. Doyle, *Communion Ecclesiology*, 59.

38. Ibid., 60.

39. De Lubac, *Catholicism*, 66.

rist, the source of the unitive force of the Eucharist is more christocentric than trinitarian. Wood astutely notes that the trinitarian source of this unity is not always as overt in de Lubac's writing as one would like to see.[40] This is due to the fact that de Lubac compares the unity of humanity to the unity of the body within a christocentric model rather than in the trinitarian one. Wood further comments that there is a strong pneumatological element in de Lubac's christocentric ecclesiology. Since the Eucharist is identified with the church, which is the body of Christ and also the body of the Spirit, then the pneumatolgocal source of the unity of the Eucharist cannot be neglected in de Lubac's ecclesiology, which is identified with the Eucharist.[41] In justice to de Lubac, one can say that the pneumatological element in his ecclesiology is subordinated to the christological.[42]

The Complementarity of Eucharistic Realism and Ecclesial Realism

In de Lubac's eucharistic ecclesiology the "complementarity" of eucharistic realism and ecclesial realism influences the institution of the church hierarchy.[43] Hans Urs von Balthasa rightly comments that de Lubac's focus lies in the complementarity by which the church constitutes the Eucharist through its hierarchical office, and the Eucharist constitutes the church as "incorporation into Christ's body."[44] De Lubac's exposition of this complementarity corrects the over-emphasis on the real presence and re-directs due attention to ecclesial realism. His insightful explanation demonstrates how the church produces the Eucharist; that though the church institutes the hierarchy to produce the Eucharist, the Eucharist as the end, defines the hierarchical power of the church. This means that the church hierarchy is not for self-perpetuation—and this is a caution against the over-institutionalization and totalitarian temptation of the church.[45] As such, de Lubac's emphasis that the Eucharist produces the church prevents the loss of the sense of the sacred with regard to the church.

Regarding how the church produces the Eucharist, de Lubac further elaborates that the priesthood of the church is instituted principally to

40. Wood, *Spiritual Exegesis*, 133.

41. Ibid., 133, 150–51.

42. Doyle, *Communion Ecclesiology*, 71.

43. Balthasar, *Theology of Henri de Lubac*, 108.

44. Ibid.

45. Grumett, *De Lubac*, 52.

produce the Eucharist.[46] He relies on the two-fold priesthood from the tradition of St. Leo the Great to maintain that the ordained priesthood is a "'particular priesthood'" within the "general priesthood."[47] The particular priesthood is also the "ministerial priesthood" designated to bishops and clergy, who have the responsibility and prerogative to produce the Eucharist. On one hand de Lubac carefully asserts the power of the ministerial priesthood that the priest who consecrates and offers the sacrifice celebrates in *persona Christi*. On the other hand, he cautions that this priesthood does not create a two-rank membership within the church. Ordination does not make the priest superior to the laity.[48] In other words, the priesthood is mediatory but not inter-mediatory between the Eucharist and the laity. The hierarchy of the church does not exist for its own sake but for the communication of the Eucharist, which is for all. The authority and hierarchy of the church should not be self-serving, but for the very purpose of the salvation and the unity of humanity in Christ.

In explaining how the Eucharist produces the church, de Lubac interprets the mystery of the Eucharist as the "mystery of communication . . .rounded out in a mystery of communion."[49] The church as the Mystical Body of Christ constitutes itself by the celebration of the mystery. De Lubac further asserts the unitive force of the mystery of the Eucharist, which turns the gathering of the "social" body of the church with the "visible pastors" for the Eucharist into the Mystical Body of Christ.[50] There shall be no break at all between the Mystical Body of Christ and the Eucharist. In other words, the mystery of unity of the church is the same as that of the Eucharist. De Lubac reiterates St Paul's teaching to support his point: "there is a 'mystical identification' between Christ and his Church, and the reality of the eucharistic presence is a guarantee for us of the 'mystical' reality of the Church."[51] Thus de Lubac concludes that the relationship between ecclesial realism and eucharistic realism is that each guarantees the other. "Ecclesial realism safeguards eucharistic realism, and the latter confirms the former."[52]

---

46. De Lubac, *Splendor*, 133.

47. Ibid., 136–37, 140.

48. Ibid., 140–41.

49. Ibid., 153.

50. Ibid.,152.

51. Ibid., 157.

52. De Lubac, *Corpus Mysticum*, 251.

The Eucharist, the Church Structure and Order

De Lubac explains how the Eucharist furnishes the basis for the relationship of the particular and local churches within the universal church.[53] He adopts the ancient liturgy of the Roman Church's Eucharist, namely the sending of *fermentum*, a piece of consecrated bread from the bishop to the priest presiding in the "titular" churches of the same city, which expressed the ecclesiastical unity.[54] This "dynamic unity" embodied by the Eucharist is significant for the relationship between the particular church and the universal church.[55] Both the *fermentum* and the bishop who sends it give the theological ground of the particular churches that each of them is a "specific instance" of the universal church. And the universal church is the "prior," concrete church of Jerusalem, but not from an "undifferentiated universal church,"[56] and also not from the church in Rome. De Lubac explains that while the particular church is fully universal as such, a local church has its own essential character or feature that distinguishes it from the universal church. For example, a local church at least has some part that is "merely human order"[57] for socio-cultural reasons, and this human order does not negate its ecclesiality. Such a socio-culturally formed human order of the local church is imperative for the universal church to take a foothold in a specific cultural context. The unity of the universal church and the particular church, and the distinction between the particular church and the local church, highlighted by de Lubac, reflect his sensitivity to diverse cultures, which is indispensable to his mission to re-engage the church with the cultural milieu.

The Cosmological Intention of the Eucharist

Though the unity of the Eucharist understood by de Lubac seems inclusive, his interpretation of the Eucharist is criticized because of his insufficient attention to the unity of the wider creation with God—in most of his work he includes only humanity in his concept of nature.[58] He does not seem

53. Grumett, *De Lubac*, 63.

54. Ibid., 57.

55. Ibid., 63.

56. Ibid.; De Lubac, *Motherhood of Church*, 207.

57. Grumett, *De Lubac*, 64.

58. Grumett, "Eucharist," 167.

to embrace unequivocally the nonhuman creation in the Eucharist. This omission can be seen in *Supernatural* and *The Mystery of the Supernatural*, in both of which de Lubac's consistent interest is only in humanity, and not in the wider creation, as the graced nature.[59]

Grumett comments that de Lubac usually identifies nature with human nature and the concept of pure nature "remains intact" in his concept of material nature.[60] Therefore, de Lubac quite often neglects the role of supernatural action in relation to the wider creation. That is why Grumett concurs with Paul McPartlan that for de Lubac, in the Eucharist there is Jesus' gathering of humanity to himself but not the material creation. Grumett also comments that the implications of de Lubac's eucharistic ecclesiology are vague in the sense that, though de Lubac intends to give an account of the Eucharist to challenge the church's fixation on the issues of definition and the presence, he seems unable to revitalize the church because of his failure to "promote and defend materialistic notions of the Eucharist."[61] The sense of sacred toward creation is thus undermined. In short, de Lubac's theology of the Eucharist faces the queries of insufficient attention to creation and the cosmological dimension.

To conclude, in de Lubac's theological interpretation, the Eucharist is the sacrament of the spiritual unity of all humanity. This expresses his high sense of Catholicism, to which de Lubac adheres throughout his theological career. His concept of the interaction between the natural and the supernatural, as well as his retrieval of the unity of the three bodies from *corpus mysticum*, form his sacramental eucharistic ecclesiology. The complementarity of ecclesial realism and eucharistic realism provides the theological ground for the church hierarchy and order.[62] Though there are doubts about the cosmological intention of the Eucharist in his interpretation, the centrality of the Eucharist in de Lubac's ecclesiology is well acknowledged.

59. De Lubac, *Brief Catechesis*, 10–11. Though in *A Brief Catechesis*, de Lubac seems to be loosening a bit on his persistence in the sole inclusion of human being into the Eucharist, it is obvious that he focuses clearly on human nature in this book.

60. Grumett, "Eucharist," 167.

61. Ibid., 172.

62. A remark must be made here that de Lubac's understanding of the church hierarchy is not representative of Catholic theology.

DE LUBAC'S ANALYSIS OF INDIVIDUALISM, TOTALITARIANISM, AND HIERARCHICAL CULTURE

Individualism

At the beginning of *Catholicism,* de Lubac addresses the issue of individualism as one of the most prevailing cultural currents in his contemporary world. He does this by first pinpointing the individualistic detachment of the church from society, and challenging the church to reflect on accusations of being individualistic.[63] De Lubac briefly comments that the individualistic errors of recent centuries were mainly caused by a general trend of individualism and admits that there was no single reason for it. Rather, he discusses at length two areas in which the church was impacted by individualism. First, the church could not offer an effective resistance to individualism. As a result, individualism infiltrated ascetics, sermons, theology, academic teaching, and especially liturgy and worship.[64] Second, de Lubac criticizes the antagonistic attitude of the church as seen first against Berengar of Tours and then the Protestants. This attitude caused the church to converge too much on eucharistic realism and severely undermined ecclesial realism, which is an essential fruit of the church's unity.[65] Thus the eucharistic piety became individualistic, focusing on one's own salvation. Consequently, faith became private, and Christians are pre-occupied with those concerns that belong to their private realms. Justice and charity are rendered as individual obligations but not the mission of the church. Such withdrawal from solidarity with others was a betrayal to the spirit of Catholicism.[66] While de Lubac criticizes the impact of individualism on the church in various places, his comments on the causes and impact of the individualistic culture outside the church are rather sporadic.

Totalitarianism and Hierarchical Culture

De Lubac is well aware of the impact of atheism and totalitarianism on the hierarchical culture in society and the church. While atheists believe

---

63. De Lubac, *Catholicism,* x–xi.

64. Ibid., 168–69.

65. De Lubac, *Theology in History,* 229.

66. Ibid., 442, 450.

that repudiation of transcendence makes immanence become complete,[67] de Lubac argues that without transcendence, "becoming" means nothing except absurdity.[68] De Lubac warns that in a "non-transcendent society" human beings will be reduced functionally to a system of social relationships to the detriment of their "personal interiority," resulting in tyranny.[69] Balthasar rightly notes that this idea of transcendence is crucial in de Lubac's theology of culture, because "a purely immanent notion of culture remains an inner contradiction . . . and that it is only the Christian with his hope beyond failure and death,"[70] who can resolve this contradiction.

While de Lubac criticizes the impact of totalitarianism on society in his contemporary world, he urges the church to be self-critical toward its own temptation to become totalitarian. The church should not be too apt to jump into protest against totalitarianism as if it were immune to this vice.[71] It must not be forgotten that after the fourteenth century, when the church had been regarded as holding "mystical powers of communion that were once ascribed to Christ's mystical body in the Eucharist,"[72] there was a transfer of not just the mystery but also power from the Eucharist to the church. The church was then heavily imbued with institutional power over both the spiritual and the temporal realms. Any exclusive claims to bring in social order by the church or some sort of over-claimed idea of the church could actually be an undue material correspondence of the church to the physical body of Christ, and could seduce the church to become totalitarian. De Lubac explains that such complete and absolute identification of the mystical body of Christ with the institution established by him has caused extreme situations that do not correspond to the true church.[73] Such material correspondence will lead to some sort of "ecclesiological monophysitism" that may overly assimilate the church with Christ.[74] This assimilation can lead to clerical totalitarianism.

67. De Lubac, *Catholicism*, 203.

68. Ibid., 202.

69. Ibid., 204.

70. Balthasar, *Theology of Henri de Lubac*, 48.

71. De Lubac, *Splendor*, 226.

72. Pecknold, "Migrations of the Host," 83.

73. De Lubac, *Paradox*, 20.

74. Ibid., 24.

DE LUBAC'S ADDRESS TO INDIVIDUALISM, TOTALITARIANISM AND HIERARCHICAL CULTURE

Individualism

In addressing individualism, de Lubac highlights the unitive force of the Eucharist against individualism in *Catholicism*.[75] De Lubac laments pervasive individualism in the general cultural milieu and the individualistic piety brought by some Protestant theologians who say that the Eucharist, as a communion of the faithful with the mysterious presence of Christ at its best scenario, is not partaking of Christ. He argues against this "subsidiary symbolism,"[76] quoting St Paschasius Radbertus of the ninth century, and defenders against Berengar of the eleventh century, all of whom would not hesitate to die in defense of the interdependence of the eucharistic realism and the unitive force of the Mystical Body on the altar.

De Lubac criticizes that the individualistic eucharistic piety of the church has been imbued with the pre-occupation of one's own salvation. This individualistic culture of the church has caused it to retreat from justice and charity. In countering individualism, he highlights the unitive force of the Eucharist against the individualistic culture in *Catholicism*.[77] His intention is to revitalize the spiritual meaning and the essential fruits of the Eucharist, that is, the unity of the church. The centrality of the Eucharist in the "overall economy of the Christian Mystery" must be made sufficiently explicit.[78] Hence, he engages in re-emphasizing the social and corporate sense of eucharistic piety that was pervasive prior to the twelfth century. Formerly the celebration of the Eucharist was predominantly a communal event. In celebrating the Eucharist, the individuals were incorporated into the Mystical Body of Christ. Therefore, de Lubac emphasizes that the sacrament of the Eucharist is an instrument of ecclesial unity.[79] Through the Eucharist a Christian is united to Christ. He specifically mentions that this union with Christ is not a "purely individual relationship between the soul and God or Christ."[80] On the contrary, this union implies the existence of a society that appears in the form of a human institution pointing to a divine

---

75. De Lubac, *Catholicism*, 174.

76. Ibid.

77. Ibid.

78. De Lubac, *Theology in History*, 229.

79. De Lubac, *Catholicism*, 51.

80. Ibid., 48

reality.[81] De Lubac's explanation is in line with the sacramental theology that the sacraments are always a social, rather than an individual means pointing to the divine.

Using the sacrament of baptism as an example, de Lubac endorses the concept of "concorporation,"[82] the doctrine that incorporation in baptism is not just an array of individual participations, but the whole church is united again in one mysterious unity. De Lubac does not apply this concorporation to the incorporation in the Eucharist. However, a conjecture may be attempted here that this concept can also be applied to the Eucharist since this rite is the completion and renewal of baptism. The concept of concorporation of the whole church into the unity of the Eucharist may help further counter the individualistic piety of this rite.

Connected to the concorporation of the whole church into the one body is the reality that the Eucharist "*realizes the Church* (emphasis original)"[83]; Christ makes himself the food of those who partake in the Eucharist. De Lubac quotes St Augustine: "I am your food, but instead of my being changed into you it is you who shall be transformed into me."[84] Each individual who partakes of the Eucharist is not just united to Christ but also to those who receive Christ. Put simply, the "Head makes the unity of the Body."[85] Therefore, de Lubac regards the unity brought by the Eucharist not as a collection of individuals united to Christ separately, but as an organic unity in which each individual is related to each other in Christ. This unity should speak and live against the individualistic and private attitude toward church life, and also the larger society in which the individualistic spirit and the "communitarian spirit" quite often exclude or limit each other.[86] De Lubac explains that the Eucharist, which belongs to the sacramental system, is the unique and divine means for the transmission of God's grace to the souls and bodies to live in society.[87] In this way, the social dimension of the Eucharist is a reminder to the faithful to mindfully live a life against the individualistic eucharistic piety. From the above discussion, it is rather obvious that de Lubac has given the impression that he puts more emphasis

81. Ibid.

82. Ibid., 49.

83. De Lubac, *Splendor*, 151.

84. De Lubac, *Catholicism*, 57.

85. De Lubac, *Splendor*, 152.

86. De Lubac, *Theology in History*, 451.

87. De Lubac, *Catholicism*, 201.

on individualism within the church and its impact on the ecclesial community. It does justice to him to say that he is more concerned with how the church has been infiltrated by the individualistic culture from outside of the church.

Totalitarian and Hierarchical Culture

De Lubac does not believe that the *onus* for the "cultural alienation of religion and theology" lies solely on the shoulders of rationalists.[88] Likewise, the blame for atheism and totalitarianism should not be put entirely on atheists. Theologians have their share of accountability for the atheistic and totalitarian culture in society.[89] The idea of the neo-Thomist theologians that pure nature and the supernatural flow harmoniously along like two parallel channels caused the church to adopt a disinterested manner toward the temporal world and culture.[90] Yet, at the same time, the church was not totally immune to the desire for political powers. The relative reticence of the church toward totalitarianism in Europe further caused it to become alienated from society. This was partly because the church wished to accrue and secure papacy power by offering limited support to fascist regimes. The exchange of favor included providing limited support to fascist regimes, especially Nazi Germany, in return for governmental help for papacy to reestablish Christian civilization. De Lubac is well aware of the vortex in Europe. Though de Lubac is critical and analytical toward totalitarianism in European society and writes on these issues in *The Drama of Human Atheist Humanism*, he does not relate the Eucharist explicitly to atheistic, totalitarian culture.

Although de Lubac does not use the Eucharist to reproach social totalitarianism, by restoring the complementarity of ecclesial realism and eucharistic realism that he advocated in his eucharistic ecclesiology, he directly addresses the church's totalitarian, hierarchical culture. In doing this, he lays the foundation of his argument that the institution of the priesthood is closely connected to the church and the Eucharist. He asserts that every Christian is certainly a priest. When he says this, he is not using it as a broad statement but in a deep and primary sense of this word. He quotes Augustine to support his point, saying, "just as we call Christians all those

88. Komonchak, "Theology and Culture," 584.

89. Buckley, *Denying and Disclosing God*, 45.

90. De Lubac, *Mystery*, 41.

who have received the mystical unction in baptism, so also we should call priests all those who are members of the one Priest."[91] The mystical body of Christ, the church, is a living community of priests. The hierarchy of priesthood is for the church but not for individuals.

The two-fold priesthood—explained by de Lubac as the general priesthood and the ministerial priesthood—can be understood as a strong reminder against the temptation of the church to become over-hierarchical. Side by side with the priesthood that operates in the Eucharist is the priesthood that offers sacrifices of piety inside the heart, which has no direct bearings on the administration of the Eucharist.[92] De Lubac reminds his readers that in the Eucharist, the priesthood of the bishop and the clergy serving with him form with him the *ordo ecclesioasticus*, which is actually not a "higher dignity in the order of the Christian's participation in the grace of Christ."[93] To de Lubac it is lucid and clear that membership in Christianity has no hierarchy in terms of sanctity. He maintains that the institution of the hierarchy should not establish two levels of church and two different categories of Christians. It is true that when the priest celebrates the cultus he receives power conferred by Christ but not delegated by the community of the faithful. For clarity's sake, he highlights a basic tenet of faith that:

> The priest is not, in virtue of his priestly ordination, more of a Christian than the ordinary believer; the Order he has received is for the sake of the Eucharist, but the Eucharist is for the sake of everyone. All are called, as from this present world, to the same divine life; and that is what makes all one in the same essential dignity, the "Christian dignity" that is a wonderful renewal of the dignity of man . . .[94]

The order received by the priests is for the unity signified by the Eucharist and not for jurisdiction and differentiation; the hierarchy of the church should refrain from excess. What is done and performed by the priest is done and performed for the whole congregation, including the priest as a whole. The priest is not above the whole congregation. There is an order of functions in relating to the sacraments and ministries, but there is no order of sanctity and status. The hierarchical power should not render

91. De Lubac, *Splendor*, 133.
92. Ibid., 136.
93. Ibid., 138.
94. Ibid., 143.

the priest a supreme status regarding every aspect of the recipient's life. The hierarchy of the church should be restricted from being self-perpetuating, which can come to the point akin to a totalitarian, hierarchical culture.

De Lubac's interpretation of church hierarchy in the eucharistic context helps discern the undue hierarchical culture and over-institutionalization of the church, which derides the Catholicity and influences the character of the church that is signified by the Eucharist. The complementarity of ecclesial and eucharistic realism is crucial in de Lubac's ecclesiology, because it opposes the reduction of the church to a mere sociological institution in imitation of the secular system. In fact, in de Lubac's analysis, the church should ever be the "source of human liberty and the mother of freedom" to free individuals from restrictions of power.[95] The church is not for, but against any power that abducts individual liberty, be it totalitarianism or hierarchical culture. The mystery of the Eucharist sustains the sacred sense of the church and is a vision of freedom against deprivation.

THE COUNTERCULTURAL FUNCTION OF THE EUCHARIST ACCORDING TO DE LUBAC'S INTERPRETATION

De Lubac's primary concern is to renew Catholicism in order to re-engage the church with culture. Therefore, the cultural significance of the Eucharist in de Lubac's system is best reflected by how he interprets this sacrament of unity against the cultures impeding Catholicism, which is the universal unity of humanity in Christ. This is both a theological and cultural endeavor countering the cultural currents that snatch people away from the spirit of Catholicism, which is not just a spiritual inclusivism but also the social and historical comprehensiveness inside and outside the church.[96] It is correct to say that in de Lubac's theology the Eucharist has a mediatory role and a unifying function that carry cultural implications.[97]

De Lubac attempts to explain the cultural significance of the Eucharist in terms of its mediatory role by connecting the supernatural to the natural. His theological premise of culture is that "a purely immanent notion of culture remains an inner contradiction . . ."[98] Without transcendence, the

95. Ibid., 172.
96. Komonchak, "Theology and Culture, 594.
97. Grumett, De Lubac, 56.
98. Balthasar, Theology of Henri de Lubac, 48.

becoming of a human being is absurd and lacks a foundation.[99] Without any correspondence between the supernatural and nature, culture stands alone, without transcendence and doomed to be meaningless, which de Lubac finds unthinkable and unacceptable. Therefore, in explaining how the Eucharist has cultural implications, de Lubac first underscores the interaction between the supernatural and human nature, thereby making it possible for mediation between transcendence and culture. Then, the Eucharist, as the sacrament *par excellence*, is culturally significant because it has a mediatory role connecting the supernatural to human nature and the world of culture; for it is through the emblems of the Eucharist that the sacrament mediates the supernatural to human nature. Put differently, the Eucharist signifies and mediates the Incarnation—the penetration of the supernatural to human nature and culture.

According to de Lubac's interpretation, the Eucharist also has a unifying function which acts contrary to the cultures that may obstruct the spirit of Catholicism, that is, the unity of humanity. The Eucharist mediates the unity of the whole of humanity in Christ, which is absolutely contrary to individualistic culture. In expounding the unifying role of the Eucharist, de Lubac utilizes the patristic teachings on the Eucharist and emphasizes it as the sacrament of unity, *sacramentum unitatis ecclesiasticae*.[100] It is through de Lubac's meticulous studies of medieval patristic writings concerning the Eucharist that this emphasis providing the unity of the "three bodies" could be established. The earthly element of the bread signifying and uniting the historical body of Christ to both the present sacramental body of Christ and the Mystical Body of Christ indicates the completion of the church in the end time. Thus, the Eucharist also unifies the salvation history by connecting the present, past, and future. Moreover, by partaking of the Eucharist, the faithful are incorporated into the church, the Mystical Body of Christ, in unity. As mentioned above, the essential fruit of the Eucharist is unity, which counteracts individualistic eucharistic piety. The cultural significance of the Eucharist in unifying the individual Christians thus often comes to the foreground of de Lubac's interpretation.

By and large, however, de Lubac's work is more precisely on the spiritual aspect of this liturgy within the church. Though Komonchak comments that de Lubac's theological agenda aims at moving the spirit of Catholicism beyond the concerns of "spiritual inclusivism" and reach out to

99. De Lubac, *Catholicism*, 200.
100. Ibid., 51.

"social and historical comprehensiveness,"[101] it does justice to de Lubac to say that he spends more effort in articulating this unifying function of the Eucharist within the ecclesial community than illustrating how this function may counter the cultural impact outside the church. Put differently, de Lubac stresses mainly the countering function of the Eucharist against individualistic piety. However, how effective is his approach to the Eucharist in reproaching individualistic culture outside the church? The church had already been infiltrated by worldly individualism. De Lubac was certainly aware of this challenge to the effectiveness of the cultural function of the Eucharist according to his interpretation, as shown by his acknowledgement that individualism is a reality that has always been a universal phenomenon encroaching on the world to which the church is not immune.[102]

The fact that the interpretation of the Eucharist by de Lubac is more valid in countering the individualistic culture within the church than in the outside world can be explained by his inadequate cultural exegesis of the phenomenon of individualism in the larger society. For instance, in his singular work, *Catholicism*, it is reasonable to expect him to discuss individualism as a pressing issue, not just within the church but also outside the church. However, his treatment of the causes of and the impact of individualism (especially the phenomenon of individualism in society) comprises some broad statements without analytical clarity.[103] He just names the individualistic phenomenon without giving an account for it, except his mentioning of original sin as a theological explanation of this cultural current.[104] It is wished that he could have unpacked the social and theological causes of individualistic culture. However, he does not elaborate on the cultural and theological frameworks that he employs to analyze individualism in society. This lack of analytical clarity may also explain his insufficient theological and ecclesiastical attention to how the Eucharist within the church may bring a countercultural formation against the world beyond her walls. Yet a conjecture may be made for him: de Lubac may have thought it rather reasonable, as a matter of strategy, to start with self-criticism and counterculture from the church in order to change the outside world.

101. Komonchak, "Theology and Culture," 594.
102. De Lubac, *Catholicism*, 168.
103. Ibid., 168.
104. Ibid., 20.

While de Lubac uses the Eucharist to counter the individualist eucharistic piety of Christians more than individualism in society, there are still some ambiguities about the validity of his theological account of the relationship between identity and differences in the Mystical Body of Christ. McPartlan criticizes de Lubac's interpretation of the unity brought by the Eucharist as no more than a "*coincident unity-of-identity* (emphasis original)."[105] He cites de Lubac as stating: "True union does not tend to dissolve into one another the beings that it brings together, but to bring them to completion by means of one another . . . . Union differentiates."[106] However, McPartlan queries whether the unity interpreted by de Lubac is actually substantiated by something people have "identically in common,"[107] for instance the same image of God in each of them. As such, differentiation cannot be complete. In such a case, the unity interpreted by de Lubac is not brought by completion through the means of one another, since there is no differentiation. McPartlan wonders whether such unity would be just a coincident unity-of-identity.[108] He further argues that the unity of human beings in Christ, according to his reading of de Lubac, does not follow the model of "circumincession" of the persons of the Trinity.[109] McPartlan's criticism against de Lubac's notion of unity boils down to this: if human beings in Christ are united because they are identically in common, and this coincident unity-of-identity does not constitute any relationships that unite them, how far can one conclude that they live as a social unity against individualistic culture? McPartlan fairly comments that though de Lubac is "seeking a unity between Christians which will distinguish them in unity and, as it were, hold them apart in unity, but he seems unable to formulate it."[110] Though de Lubac once mentioned "coincidence is no more union than proximity is presence. There is no real unity without persisting difference,"[111] and he suggests that human beings are brought to union and completion by means of each other by submitting themselves to God,[112] yet he quite leaves the theological details of this completion by means of each

---

105. McPartlan, *Eucharist that Makes the Church*, 19.

106. Ibid.

107. Ibid.

108. Ibid.

109. Ibid., 92.

110. Ibid., 93.

111. De Lubac, *Catholicism*, 190.

112. Ibid., 184.

other undeveloped. Therefore, the validity of de Lubac's interpretation of the Eucharist in the formation of countering the individualistic culture is undermined by his lack of explanation of the relationship between sameness and differences in the unity of humanity. As individualism usually stresses the distinctiveness that often leads to separation, de Lubac's lack of interpretation of the Eucharist in relation to the differences weakens the validity of the Eucharist in countering individualistic culture.

Regarding the totalitarian and hierarchical culture, de Lubac mainly focuses on urging the church to be self-critical to its tendency to being over-hierarchical, which can lead to clerical totalitarianism. He, however, does not explain how the Eucharist may address totalitarianism in society. With respect to the hierarchical culture, de Lubac's mutuality of ecclesial realism and eucharistic realism elucidates quite clearly that the hierarchy of the church is instituted for the Eucharist as its end. The power of the priesthood should be given and defined at the same time by Christ in consecrating the bread and the wine. The two-fold aspect of the general priesthood and the ministerial priesthood should create no two-tier membership in the church. It is true that while the church produces the Eucharist, the Eucharist prescribes the power of the church. Because of the identity of the mystery of the church and the Eucharist, the church should not be downgraded to become a social institution that follows the secular system. As such, de Lubac's theological interpretation of the Eucharist with respect to the hierarchical culture of the church sounds theologically valid and relevant.

However, one may challenge that though the Roman Catholic Church has been celebrating the Eucharist for centuries, it has also been perceived as totalitarian and hierarchical. De Lubac's interpretation of the Eucharist against totalitarian and hierarchical culture seems to be a kind of subculture or even private opinion only within the church itself, not to mention within the culture of the larger society. This may be a vivid example of what is theologically valid but may not be ecclesiastically effective automatically. Yet caution must also be taken here that what is ineffective in theological interpretation cannot lead to ecclesiastical effectiveness in general. Nevertheless, de Lubac's theological explanation of the Eucharist with respect to totalitarianism and hierarchical culture should become the self-critical spirit of the church to strive to live honestly according to the *ethos* of the Eucharist, which can be countercultural.

SUMMARY

In this chapter, the centrality of the Eucharist in de Lubac's sacramental ecclesiology is outlined. Special attention is given to how de Lubac's concept of natural-supernatural, in which nature and the supernatural are not separated completely, lays the foundation of the cultural significance of the Eucharist. According to this concept, the Eucharist has a mediatory role: through its symbols it mediates the supernatural to nature and the world of culture. Besides this mediatory role, the Eucharist has a unifying function that unites the whole of humanity in Christ. This unifying role is the fundamental basis of the Eucharist in countering individualism, against which de Lubac speaks strongly. In addition to individualism, he also advocates against the totalitarian and hierarchical cultures. Yet, he is not explicit enough in elaborating how the Eucharist may resist totalitarianism inside and outside the church. He, however, makes a theologically sound interpretation of the Eucharist in discerning and resisting the hierarchical culture by explaining that the Eucharist is for all, and it denies any differentiation in sanctity and dignity within the church. Though de Lubac attempts to give a theological account of how the Eucharist counters the totalitarian and hierarchical culture, the church has been subject to queries concerning these two issues within its polity for a long time. One may observe that de Lubac's intention to revitalize eucharistic practice and re-interpret it in order to "subvert or counteract" cultural current in the mid-twentieth century may not be as valid and effective as he expects, especially when the totalitarian and hierarchical cultural currents are involved both inside and outside the church.[113] Nonetheless, he does play a pioneering role in re-kindling interest in the studies of the Eucharist, and interpreting the Eucharist as a countercultural liturgy in the twentieth century.

---

113. Hollon, *Everything is Sacred*, 57.

4

John Zizioulas's Interpretation of the Eucharist

Countering the Exploitive Culture on Nature and Individualism

INTRODUCTION

JOHN ZIZIOULAS (1931–), the Metropolitan of Pergamon, has a strong reputation of active engagement in ecumenical circles. He started researching the Eucharist and conciliar structures in the early years of his theological career. He also participates in ecumenical conversations concerning cultural currents. Besides these, he is renowned for his neo-patristic studies and writings on personhood. His book *Being as Communion* is the first crystallization of this neo-patristic synthesis on personhood and the church. In this book, Zizioulas explicates the inextricable connection between person and communion by elaborating the patristic ontology of personhood, and weaves the implications of this connection with the Eucharist, which mandates the structure and life of the eucharistic community.

This chapter focuses on how Zizioulas interprets the theology of the Eucharist in relation to cultural currents pinpointed by him, namely; the exploitive culture on nature and individualism; and how valid his interpretation can be in countering these two cultural currents. This examination will begin with Zizioulas's doctrine of the Trinity as a portal to understand his interpretation of the Eucharist. His doctrine of the Trinity is chosen as a starting point for three reasons. First, according to Zizioulas, the trinitarian doctrine is crucial to conferring meaning on the lives of ordinary people. He maintains that Christian faith becomes void of all significance to humanity if it cannot be connected with the doctrine of the Trinity.[1] Second, based on the patristic teachings, Zizioulas argues that the trinitarian doctrine is decisive for ecclesiology, which is inseparable from the Eucharist. Both the Eucharist and the church constitute each other, and they are modeled after the "Trinitarian way of existence."[2] Third, the doctrine of the Trinity constitutes personhood, which is crucial to anthropology and every concern of humankind. Zizioulas's system of the trinitarian doctrine has significant impact both at the social and personal levels. Therefore, this chapter will examine his interpretation of the Eucharist in relation to the world and personhood, considering how he counters the abusive impact of the cultural current on creation and individualism by offering a eucharistic worldview and an *ethos* of otherness embodied in the Eucharist.[3]

ZIZIOULAS'S INTERPRETATION OF THE EUCHARIST

The Personal-Hypostatic Doctrine of the Trinity

Zizioulas highlights the difference between the trinitarian doctrine of the West and the East. He rejects western trinitarian doctrine, which is based on *ousia*. He argues that this kind of trinitarian doctrine makes the Trinity secondary to the impersonal substance *ousia*, since "what is shared is prior to what shares in it."[4] Zizioulas challenges the subordination of the Trinity to *ousia* by tracing the Cappadocian Fathers' personal-hypostatic ontology of the Trinity.[5] He underscores Gregory of Nyssa's teaching that the cause of the trinitarian existence of God is the Father, not the impersonal substance shared by the three persons.[6] In the personal-hypostatic doctrine of the Trinity, the Father causes the other two persons to exist (outside the frame-

1. Zizioulas, *One and Many*, 6.
2. Ibid., 15.
3. Zizioulas, *Eucharistic Communion and World*, 123.
4. Zizioulas, *One and Many*, 10.
5. Ibid., 29.
6. Ibid., 22.

work of time) while they condition the Father. The three persons exist in communion because of the perfect love among themselves. In other words, their being is not caused by essence shared among them and is inseparable from their relationship. Zizioulas asserts there is no naked being or bare essence as such. They are beings existing as persons in communion. Because of love for the other, the three persons are in perfect communion without diminishing each other's particularity and uniqueness. The Cappadocian Fathers stress that the hypostases of the Trinity are "modes of existence," meaning "the Father is unbegotten, the Son as begotten, and the Holy Spirit as proceeding all connote exclusively ways in which those Persons are in existence and have their being."[7] Furthermore, he argues that though human beings can know God through the economic Trinity, the economic Trinity does not exhaust the immanent Trinity.[8] While Zizioulas appreciates the theological account for demonstrating the relevance of the Trinity to human beings by certain theologians (for example, Jürgen Moltmann), he does not agree with Karl Rahner, who has collapsed the immanent Trinity into the economic Trinity. To Zizioulas, the immanent Trinity is immutable, and only with the aid of apophatic theology can one go beyond the economic Trinity.[9] Thus, He maintains the distinction between the immanent Trinity and the economic Trinity.

The Impact of the Trinity on the Eucharist and the Church

As mentioned above, Zizioulas is deeply concerned with the relevance of the Trinity to the lives of ordinary people. He further explains that without a proper doctrine of the Trinity, there cannot be an ecclesiology. Conversely, a proper ecclesiology can make the trinitarian doctrine relevant to the needs of the world.[10] A proper ecclesiology is crucial, since human beings actualize their personhood in the church, which offers people a foretaste of the eschatological communion with the triune God.[11] Based on the patristic tradition, Zizioulas maintains that the Eucharist, which is the communion of God and the sacrament of the foretaste of *eschaton*, is inextricably connected to the doctrine of Trinity and ecclesiology. Both the

7. Ibid., 29.

8. Zizioulas, *Communion and Otherness*, 201.

9. Ibid., 203.

10. Zizioulas, *One and Many*, 15.

11. Ibid.

church and the Eucharist have to embody the trinitarian way of existence of the triune God, that is, *koinonia* or communion with God.[12] Besides, the church and the Eucharist mutually constitute each other. Put differently, the doctrine of the Trinity circumscribes the ways of structuring both the Eucharist and the church, and they mutually constitute each other.[13] Below is the explanation of how the Trinity impacts the structures of the Eucharist and the church, and the relationship between them.

First, the Trinity is a communion that makes the Eucharist a communion as well, which is also called the Holy Communion. In the Orthodox tradition, the Holy Communion is not about things. The Eucharist is *synaxis*, a "gathering in one place" of all people in the Eucharist.[14] It represents the eschatological Kingdom of God, which is a gathering of the dispersed people to one place (Matt 13:47; 1 Cor 11:20–23). Because the Eucharist is a communion of God's people, the practice of private mass without the laity, or the Eucharist which includes only a particular kind of people, be it by natural difference or social division, is unthinkable and unacceptable to Zizioulas.[15]

Zizioulas stresses that ecclesiology has to be based on trinitarian theology. Since the triune God is a communion, the result is the ecclesiology of communion. First and foremost, the church is a *koinonia* or a communion of God. Zizioulas explains that this genitive "of" denotes that the identity of the church stemmed from the personal relationship or communion with God.[16] The *koinonia* or sharing in communion with God is through the synthesis of Christology and Pneumatology, that is, the incorporation of the church in God through Christ by the power of the Holy Spirit.[17] Besides the assertion that the Trinity constitutes both the Eucharist and the church as communion of God, Zizioulas emphasizes the ecclesiological implication of the Eucharist.

Second, Zizioulas emphasizes that the communion of the three persons in the Trinity maintains the primordial "one" and the "many." This

12. Ibid., 15, 51.

13. Zizioulas, *Eucharistic Communion and World*, 105.

14. Ibid., 46–47.

15. De Lubac, *Splendor*, 151. The position of Zizioulas in this issue is different from that of de Lubac. De Lubac does not regard the Eucharist as *synaxis* or assembly. For de Lubac, the Eucharist can be either a large gathering or just a person attending it.

16. Zizioulas, *One and Many*, 51–52.

17. Ibid., 51.

unity is maintained without demolishing the many in the Trinity through the personal loving relationship among the persons, but not through the impersonal *ousia*. Zizioulas explains that this relational "the-one-and-the-many" is demonstrated in the celebration of the Eucharist. In the Liturgy, the bishop is surrounded by the presbyters and all the orders, including the laity. The unity of the many of the Trinity is represented by the episcopal oneness of the bishop who presides over the Eucharist. His stance on this point is supported in his book, *Eucharist, Bishop, Church*. In this book, Zizioulas did a laborious study to illustrate and prove the point that the bishop, through presiding in the Eucharist, represents the unity of the church in the consciousness of the primitive church at least in the first three centuries. This book can explain why he is almost intransigent regarding the leadership of the bishop in the Eucharist and the unity of the church. However, his position on the presidency of the bishop in the Eucharist and the church *ordo* is questioned by Miroslav Volf and also Nicholaos Loudovikos. Their queries will be addressed later in chapter 6.

Therefore, the episcopal presidency of the Eucharist is central to Zizioulas's ecclesiology, especially to the catholicity and relation between the local church and the universal church. Since the bishop is ordained by more than one bishop, "his ministry transcends *the local community*" (emphasis original).[18] The bishop makes the local church catholic and an autocephaly. He is the link between the local church and the universal church.[19] In other words, the catholicity of the Eucharist is embodied by the presidency of the bishop, *alter apostolus* who connects the local churches through all ages.[20] The catholicity of the church is also revealed and actualized in the Eucharist, albeit the ultimate catholicity is an eschatological reality.[21]

In close connection with catholicity, Zizioulas also emphasizes the-one-and-the-many in the Eucharist and the bishop. What happens in the Last Supper is repeated in the Eucharist. When the many take the one bread, they become one, and the one body of Christ contains many (1 Cor 10:16–17) through the Holy Spirit. That is why Christ is a corporate personality in which the one and the many coincide.[22] The one-and-the-many is also true of the bishop, who is "the ecclesiological presupposition *par*

18. Zizioulas, *Eucharistic Communion and World*, 108.

19. Zizioulas, *One and Many*, 259.

20. Ibid., 241.

21. Zizioulas, *Being as Communion* 144–45.

22. Zizioulas, *One and Many*, 142.

excellence of the Eucharist" representing Christ, the *alter christus*,[23] and preserving the eschatological dimension of the church.

In Zizioulas's eucharistic ecclesiology, the catholicity of the local church should not be understood as independence from other local churches. Zizioulas has reservations about Nicholas Afanassieff's suggestion that "wherever the Eucharist is, there is the Church,"[24] because this may lead to a misunderstanding that the local church has priority over the universal church. Zizioulas arugues that in the Orthodox world, each local church is related to each other through the bishop, as previously mentioned. Put simply, the unity of the Orthodox Church hinges on the bishop. The conciliarity of the Orthodox Church is structured to balance the autonomy of the local church and the wholeness of the universal church. In councils, bishops convene to make decisions in consensus on issues common to their churches. However, no bishop can intervene in issues particular to another local church.[25]

Thus, Zizioulas's explanation of the communion, or the relational one-and-the-many of the Trinity, demonstrates how the Trinity is embodied in the structure of the Eucharist and the church, as well as the crucial importance of the Eucharist on the ecclesial community. He makes his position about the relation between the church and the Eucharist very clear by saying: "My position, which I wish to develop here, is that *the Church constitutes the Eucharist while being constituted by it* (emphasis original). Church and Eucharist are inter-dependent; they coincide, and are even in some sense *identical* (emphasis added)."[26] He states unequivocally that the structure of the Eucharist prescribes the structure of the church, and the ministries in the Eucharist become the most significant ministries of the church.[27]

Third, Zizioulas reminds his readers that the trinitarian doctrine should be relevant to the needs of the world. The most fundamental ground of the relevance of the Trinity to the world is the triune God's desire to have communion with the whole world, that is, recapitulation. This relevance constitutes the mission of the church, which is relational, meaning to establish relationship, because the Incarnation vivifies this desire of God to

23. Zizioulas, *Eucharistic Communion and World*, 108.

24. Zizioulas, *Being as Communion*, 25.

25. Zizioulas, *Lectures*, 142–43.

26. Zizioulas, *Eucharistic Communion and World*, 105.

27. Zizioulas, *One and Many*, 311.

embrace both nonhuman creation and humanity.[28] Thus, being the Body of Christ, the church engages in building a relationship between God and the world by recapitulating all creation to God through the Eucharist. And Christ is revealed as the life and recapitulation of all creation in the Eucharist.[29] In the Liturgy, the material world is brought to the church in the form of the basic elements of ordinary life and also the everyday mundane of the participants.[30] The Eucharist best embodies the relationality of the Trinity with nonhuman creation through *anaphora* and the "priestly function of the human being creation,"[31] which stem from the eucharistic worldview that treats the cosmos as a liturgy rather than as dualistic. The Eucharist also represents the recapitulation of humanity to the triune God through the *ethos* of otherness, which will be discussed in the later part of this chapter.

The Eucharist and the Eucharistic Worldview

Zizioulas underscores that in the Orthodox Church, the Eucharist is the "most positive and active acceptance of the world and creation."[32] The Eucharist is not solely concerned with humanity; it has a cosmic dimension. In the Orthodox tradition, the Eucharist is an event that celebrates a particular vision of the world, namely the "eucharistic vision of the world."[33] It was particularly reflected in the historical study that in the ancient church, when believers went to the Eucharist, they carried along some of the fruits of creation, which were "paraded" in the liturgical procession. The bishop finally received those gifts from them and lifted them up to God as Eucharist, or *eucharistia*, meaning thanksgiving.[34] The receiving and lifting up of the gifts is also known as *anaphora*. In the ancient church, *eucharistia*

28. Ibid., 57.

29. Zizioulas, *Being as Communion,* 119.

30. Zizioulas, *One and Many,* 57.

31. Zizioulas, *Communion and Otherness,* 96; *Eucharistic Communion and World,* 137. Based on St. Maximus the Confessor's idea of prince of creation, Zizioulas develops the notion of priest of creation to represent the priesthood of the church and the faithful.

32. Zizioulas, *Eucharistic Communion and World,* 125.

33. Ibid., 124. Before going into the cosmic dimension of the Eucharist, Zizioulas clears up the misunderstandings about the Eucharist. First the Eucharist should not be seen as an object or thing that had caused debates like transubstantiation or eucharistic realism. Second, the Eucharist should not be objectified as a means of grace.

34. Ibid.

and *anaphora* were used interchangeably to refer to the Eucharist because they were the primary focus of the Liturgy. Both terms entail the accepting and affirmative attitude of the eucharistic community toward creation. Besides the Eucharist sanctifies and purifies the gifts, which come from and represent nature returned to the Creator, it is deemed as "a medicine of immortality" to the material world.[35] In the Eucharist, the material world is not despised or subjugated by human beings for their own good. Instead, it is lifted up and acknowledged as part and parcel of human existence in the world. As such, the Eucharist enlightens humanity on a different way of relating to nature. Nature and humanity are actually inseparable and indispensable to each other's existence. Zizioulas's eucharistic worldview can also be regarded as, in Santmire's words, "ritualizing nature,"[36] which means to interpret nature as seen from the context of the liturgy. The eucharistic worldview or interpretation of the world highlighted by Zizioulas is the purging of the demarcation between the natural and the supernatural. Because of the holistic eucharistic vision of the world, there is no such dichotomy.[37] All are sanctified and recapitulated to the Creator in the Eucharist. At the altar, where the faithful assemble, the cosmological dimension of the Eucharist is manifested by the recapitulation of creation to God through the Holy Spirit as a foretaste of the *eschaton*.

Zizioulas further explains that the recapitulation of creation is done through a human being who is the "priest of creation."[38] Humanity's responsibility is to make nature capable of having communion, since God intends the whole creation to be in communion with himself. However, mortal creation can only be in communion with the immortal God through human beings. Humanity is the species that is organically connected with nature because they share the materiality of nature. Furthermore, they are given the mission from God to recapitulate the whole creation to him.[39] Due to the shared materiality with creation and the God-given purpose to unite the world, a human being is capable of being the priest of creation in the Eucharist to recapitulate nature through the Holy Spirit.

Zizioulas develops the notion of the priest of creation and applies it to the eucharistic community, the church. Because of the organic link to

---

35. Ibid., 125.

36. Santmire, *Ritualizing Nature*, 4.

37. Zizioulas, *Eucharistic Communion and World*, 126.

38. Ibid., 137.

39. Zizioulas, *Lectures*, 89.

creation and also the capacity to unite the world, a human being can act as a priest of creation, as can the church, which is the Body of Christ.[40] In the Eucharist, the bishop and the assembly together act as the priest of creation by lifting up gifts and offering prayers (*anaphora*) to God in communion. This lifting up of gifts by the priest of creation is an acknowledgement of the Other, who gives the existence of many others, including ourselves, as gifts. Thus, besides embodying a worldview with respect to nature, the Eucharist is also a communion of others.

This acknowledgement of others in the Eucharist is closely related to the communion and otherness in Zizioulas's theological system. Nonna Verna Harrison notes in Zizioulas's writings that this priestly vocation of human beings is equivalent to the "actualization of truly personal existence,"[41] which is constituted by freely affirming other beings. Communion and otherness originate in the Holy Trinity and establish personhood, which is significant for every single need of humanity. One of the results is that the Eucharist affirms otherness.

The Eucharist Is an Affirmation of Otherness

Zizioulas stresses that the Eucharist is where "communion and otherness are realized *par excellence*."[42] This meeting and coinciding of communion and otherness in the Eucharist is based on the communion of the persons in the Holy Trinity and the hypostasization of the person of Christ. According to patristic tradition, the Father is the person (*hypostasis*) who is the *monarchia*, the one cause of the Trinity. The Father in his absolute freedom causes the persons of the Son and the Holy Spirit to be and to have communion with him. This causality or *arche* is relational and outside the category of time. It means that the Father is ontologically with the Son and the Spirit. It is inconceivable to speak of the Father without these two. As such, God is one and three at the same time. Therefore, the Trinity is the primordial the-one-and-the-many. Zizioulas further explains that the three persons exist as absolute otherness to each other while they are in communion with each other. Zizioulas states that in this primordial communion, the *monarchia* of the Father secures and maintains the oneness of the Trinity without purging the otherness of the other persons. The three persons in com-

40. Ziziouas, *Eucharistic Communion and World*, 137.

41. Harrison, "Zizioulas on Communion," 292.

42. Zizioulas, *Communion and Otherness*, 7.

munion are absolutely free and in the Trinity there is freedom for others. That is, other persons are allowed in as they are. Hence, the communion is constitutive of otherness and does not jeopardize it.[43] Zizioulas highlights that based on the Trinity the Eucharist is the "ontological affirmation of otherness and particularity."[44] In the patristic tradition, the Other is both the cause of particularity and ultimate destination of the particular beings, that is, their "rest."[45] And the Other can be understood as an "ever-moving rest,"[46] which sounds quite like an oxymoron. It actually refers to moving from one particularity to another without negating the particularity. Each one in the ever-moving rest affirms the particularity of the others. Where the otherness and particularity are confirmed there is rest and communion. It is imperative to point out that in Zizioulas's theology, the Trinity as a communion of otherness has significant implications on the personhood and the Eucharist, which is explained below.

Zizioulas employs two terms to explain what characterizes personhood: *hypostasis* and *ek-stasis*.[47] Through *hypostasis* and *ek-stasis*, individuals become persons. In patristic thought, *hypostasis* is relational. This is a mode of existence that is constitutive of being. *Hypostasis* is christological, because there are no hypostases without hypostasization in the one and unique *hypostasis* of the Son, who is the unique *hypostasis* of the Father (Heb 1:3). This christological hypostasization is extended to humanity because of the love, *eros* of the Father, which is shared within the communion of the Trinity. Zizioulas further explains that hypostasization is also pneumatological because it takes place in the Holy Spirit. Hypostasization occurs in freedom (2 Cor 3:17) and communion (*koinonia*; 2 Cor 13:13). In the Eucharist, the hypostasization of the Son and the Holy Spirit gives all the hypostases their otherness and uniqueness in love and perfect freedom, which do not exclude each other, but give a taste of their eschatological state of existence.[48]

Ek-stasis, another aspect of personhood, can be understood as the coming forward of God, who is love. Within the communion of otherness among the Trinity, each person moves out to love each of the others and

43. Ibid., 5.

44. Ibid., 79.

45. Ibid., 53.

46. Ibid.

47. Russell, "Relational Anthropology, 172–73.

48. Zizioulas, *Communion and Otherness*, 76.

allows them to exist as other in freedom. In the hypostasization previously mentioned, the beings receive this *ekstaticness* and are able to overcome the boundaries around oneself and reach out to others. Therefore, e*k-stasis* is the confirmation of *hypostasis* as other.[49] Because of *ek-stasis*, existence and otherness of oneself are confirmed through others relationally. Without *ek-stasis*, personhood vanishes. Zizioulas suggests that the *ek-stasis* that overflows from the communion of Trinity is inclusive regardless of moral or natural qualities. The Eucharist embodies this inclusive communion of the Trinity in which otherness and uniqueness are upheld because of their "ontological particularity and integrity."[50] Therefore, the Eucharist is called "the most anti-individualistic act of the Church."[51]

The Asymmetry of Otherness in the Trinity and the Hierarchy of the Church and the Eucharist

Besides explaining how the communion of otherness in the Trinity impacts cosmology and personhood, Zizioulas points out that the communion of otherness in the Trinity also prescribes an asymmetric structure of the church and the Eucharist. He explains that the communion in the Trinity is not egalitarian but asymmetric. Because throughout all the biblical and patristic references to the Trinity, there is an ordering or *taxis*: the Father always comes first, the Son second, and the Spirit third.[52] This order is outside the concept of time and absolutely cannot be altered. The *monarchia* of the Father is in fact an asymmetrical relationship. Zizioulas supports this order by the explanation of Gregory Nazianzen that the Trinity is a movement initiated by a person, the Father to the other persons.[53] This *monarchia* causation is not a matter of difference in nature, *ousia*, which is always common to the three persons. Zizioulas employs the Cappadocian argument that the Trinity shares and maintains the same *ousia* and the Father causes the Son to exist; the hypostasization of *ousia* "was and is simultaneous with personal differentiation."[54] Yet, Zizioulas emphasizes *monarchia* more than the sharing of the same *ousia*. He argues that the

49. Zizioulas, *One and Many*, 404.

50. Zizioulas, *Communion and Otherness*, 86.

51. Zizioulas, *Eucharistic Communion and World*, 128.

52. Zizioulas, *Communion and Otherness*, 137.

53. Ibid., 119.

54. Ibid., 129, n. 52.

asymmetry in the Trinity given by *monarchia* is the way in which the three persons relate to each other in the Trinity. It is about the "how" of being but not the "what" of being (*ousia*). He further contests that this asymmetry in the Trinity is ontological, not referring to any order of value or importance, be it moral or functional.[55]

Zizioulas argues that unlike any other asymmetry of power or relationships in society that may occur with pejorative connotations, the asymmetric hierarchy caused by *monarchia* does not impede communion in the Trinity. On the contrary, the *monarchia* maintains the communion of the Trinity, which is love and freedom. This is because the Father, who is "*the ultimate ontological principle of divine personhood*"[56] (emphasis original), does not destroy ontological equality by differentiating the persons in the Trinity.

Then, Zizioulas explains how the asymmetry in the Trinity has implications for ecclesiology and the Eucharist. First, he argues that the hierarchical structure of the church does not necessarily threaten communion and otherness. He upholds the ecclesiology in which hierarchical structures are essential to the church as long as they are based on the trinitarian model.[57] Order, or *taxis,* is essential in the sense that the hierarchical structures have to follow the trinitarian model, meaning they "generate otherness and respect particularity."[58] Given the scope of this chapter, it suffices to underscore that Zizioulas supports the ecclesiology that requires the structure of the church and ministries to have their roots and rationale in the trinitarian model. Second, Zizioulas also points out that there is an asymmetrical hierarchy in the Eucharist: the bishop becomes the eucharistic community's father in the image of the Father in the Trinity. Zizioulas explains this image:

> Ecclesial fatherhood reflects Trinitarian Fatherhood in that membership in the Church requires 'generation' or 'birth' or 'regeneration', which is given 'from above' in an act or event (Baptism) of *sonship* (emphasis original), that is, our acceptance by the Father as his sons by grace through our incorporation into his only-begotten Son whom he eternally generates. The Eucharist is the fulfillment and 'enjoyment' of this baptismal incorporation, and in

55. Ibid., 139.
56. Ibid., 130.
57. Ibid., 146.
58. Ibid.

this sense it is a movement from the Father through the Son in the Holy Spirit, reaching us in order to be returned by us in the same way to the Father.[59]

This, together with the concept of *monarchia*, helps explain why Zizioulas supports the asymmetric hierarchy of the church and the Eucharist, especially the centrality of episcopacy in the ecclesiology. Furthermore, Zizioulas reckons that *monarchia* causes the *taxis* of the immanent Trinity, thereby ordering the economic Trinity, which in turn directs the structure of the church and the Eucharist.[60]

In the final analysis, it is not difficult to see how the trinitarian doctrine has impacted Zizioulas's interpretation of the Eucharist, which is inextricably connected to the church. Zizioulas insists on the mutual constitution of the Eucharist and the church, and the almost automatic application of the episcopal-centric structure of the Eucharist to the church. Based on the patristic tradition of *anaphora* and the priest of creation, he also connects the Eucharist to cosmology for the mission of bringing the whole world into communion with God through humanity. This human capacity to recapitulate the creation is based on personhood, which originates from the communion of otherness in the Trinity. He also demonstrates how *monarchia* in the Trinity accounts for the hierarchy of the Eucharist and the church, basically the presence of the bishop. By connecting the trinitarian doctrine and the Eucharist with ecclesiology, cosmology, and anthropology, Zizioulas argues that the Trinity has deep relevance to the world. As such, it is no exaggeration to comment that Zizioulas's trinitarian interpretation of the Eucharist integrates and supports almost all the significant aspects of his whole theological system. Therefore, the Eucharist is of cardinal importance in Zizioulas's theology.

ZIZIOULAS'S ANALYSIS OF THE EXPLOITIVE CULTURE ON NATURE AND INDIVIDUALISM

The Exploitive Culture on Nature

In 1989, in his lectures presented at King's College London, Zizioulas had already proclaimed resolutely that the ecological problem is a "crisis of

---

59. Ibid., 148.
60. Ibid., 149.

culture."[61] As a matter of fact, his concern with the relation between theology and creation was demonstrated in his very first post-doctoral publication from 1966, "The Eucharistic Vision of the World and Contemporary Humanity."[62] Though these two publications are almost twenty-four years apart, he consistently names the cause of ecological crisis as a cultural one. His criticism is that the dualistic mindset in western theology (especially Protestant theology) has demarcated the sacred and the profane. This dualism, or dualistic worldview, has attributed to ecological problems. Note also in *The Eucharistic Communion and the World*, Zizioulas reiterates that ecological crisis is a cultural crisis. He sees the root cause of the problem as the vanishing of the sacrality of nature in culture,[63] which is precisely inculcated by the above-mentioned dualistic mindset. This loss of sacrality gives rise to the domineering or even the exploitative cultural trend to use nature for the benefit of human beings. In respect of environmental issues, Zizioulas is particularly concerned with the model of stewardship, which singles out humanity as the lord and proprietor of creation. This model was shaped by the anthropology of the Enlightenment, that humanity is master of nature, and also by the Calvinist tradition of subduing and dominating creation. The superiority of humanity over nature turns out to be a managerial or even exploitive mentality and behavior toward nature that is accountable for the ecological crisis.[64] Zizioulas also agrees with Max Weber's analysis that without the impact of the religious idea of stewardship, it would be hard to account for the ecological crisis.[65]

According to Zizioulas, the ecological crisis is a global concern that devastates all of humanity. Its impact is not just about the human community but also the well-being of creation as a whole. He even regards the ecological crisis as evil because of its overwhelming destructive power. Given the scale and the depth of this crisis, Zizioulas asserts that no single model or approach may save us. Because his analysis holds the root cause of ecological crisis to be cultural, Zizioulas suggests that a cultural approach is indispensable to tackle this concern. He also argues that to a great extent the church and theology should take responsibility for the ecological crisis and should not remain silent. They should contribute constructively

---

61. Zizioulas, "Preserving God's Creation," 5.

62. Fox, *God as Communion*, 55.

63. Zizioulas, *Eucharistic Communion and World*, 174.

64. Ibid., 133–34.

65. Ibid., 133.

to relieve the problem.[66] In contributing his own share as a theologian, he proposes that a new cultural current that stemmed from the patristic tradition of the priest of creation in the Eucharist is a promising way to alleviate the ecological crisis.

Individualism

In addition to the effect of exploitive culture on creation, Zizioulas is well aware of the individualistic culture. In particular, Zizioulas is more concerned with the impact of individualism on today's ecclesiastical life. He is anxious about the possibility of individualistic piety and pride through ascetic practices, which may breed "spiritual elitism and individualism."[67] To Zizioulas, this kind of spiritual superiority and religious individualism makes people seek individual salvation and renders the need for the church or parish superfluous. He further warns that on the very backbone of individualism is self-love, which fuels spiritual superiority.

Besides making observations and comments on individualism in the church, Zizioulas explains that this culture can be reckoned as fear of others. It is an exclusive attitude towards others in society. Zizioulas further suggests, "the fear of other is pathologically inherent in our existence and results in the fear not only of the other but of *all otherness*" (emphasis original).[68] Difference can mean divisions. When the fear of other becomes the fear of otherness to the extent that difference causes division, individualism triumphs. Zizioulas explains that the fear of otherness has cultural implication simply because respect for otherness has been an important principle in civilized societies. When there is a lack of some sort of communion for otherness, it is difficult to "produce a satisfactory culture."[69] Thus, he proposes an *ethos* of otherness to counter individualism.[70]

---

66. Ibid., 143.

67. Zizioulas, *Eucharistic Communion and World*, 82.

68. Zizioulas, *Communion and Otherness*, 2–3.

69. Ibid., 14.

70. Ibid., 88.

ZIZIOUAS'S ADDRESS TO THE EXPLOITATIVE CULTURE ON NATURE AND INDIVIDUALISM

The Exploitive Culture on Nature

Zizioulas proposes an *ethos* based on the patristic tradition of *anaphora* and the priest of creation in the Eucharist to counter the abusive culture on creation, which is chiefly responsible for the ecological crisis. He explains that mere ethics or legal rules are not adequate in countering this cultural current because it is insufficient to address ecological issues by appealing to human reason *per se*. Since the ecological crisis is a cultural issue mainly caused by the exploitive mindset toward God's creation, he suggests that a new culture is necessary to counter the abusive attitude toward nature. Zizioulas suggests that human beings need a new culture formed through liturgical experience.[71] The liturgical experience in the Eucharist nurtures the eucharistic vision of the world, which is holistic and is in sharp contrast with the abusive attitude toward nature.

Disagreeing with the western tradition that dichotomizes sacred and profane, which causes a utilitarian and exploitive attitude toward creation, Zizioulas praises the patristic tradition in which the Eucharist embraces the holistic worldview, which is the most active and positive acceptance of the world. He describes this positive approach to creation as the Liturgy *per se* being a journey in which all the faithful carry along the world with them.[72] He notes that in the earliest eucharistic prayers of the church, there is a strong sense of "the goodness of creation."[73] His observation can be supported by, for example, parts of the eucharistic prayer contained in the *Strasbourg Papyrus*: "All things you made through your wisdom . . . Jesus Christ, through whom to you . . . giving thanks, we offer . . ."[74] Taken together this all has a strong cosmological tenor. Zizioulas describes how this tenor was reflected by the faithful in the ancient church: they brought with them bread, wine and oil as gifts of creation to the Liturgy. As the head of the Liturgy, the bishop received their gifts into his hands after they had paraded them in the procession of the Liturgy. Then, the bishop lifted up the gifts and offered them back (*anaphora*) to the Creator God as Eucharist, *eucharistia* (thanksgiving).

71. Zizioulas, *Eucharistic Communion and World*, 145.

72. Ibid., 125.

73. Fox, *God as Communion*, 59.

74. See Ray, "The Strasbourg Papyrus," 47.

Zizioulas adds that the Eucharist, as it was taught in the ancient church, is primarily a thanksgiving, which has two layers of meaning. First it is an important thankful acknowledgement of the existence of the Creator God who is the utmost significant gift.[75] Second, it is an act of thanksgiving to the givenness of creation, including human beings. What Zizioulas notes about *eucharistia* is also supported by Denis Edwards: the *anaphora* (lifting up and giving back) prayer of St. Basil and also that of St. John Chrysostom were praises of the God of all creation.[76] Zizioulas further proves that in some cases of *Mystagogical Catecheses*, such as the eucharistic liturgy of St. Cyril of Jerusalem, the *eucharistia* for creation was the only point of the eucharistic teaching; there was no trace of the passion of Christ.[77] This explains why such names for the Eucharist as *eucharistia* and *anaphora* were both used in the Liturgy of the ancient church, as they were the primary focus in celebrating the Eucharist.

Therefore, *anaphora*, the receiving from and offering back of gifts to God, reflects the unreserved acceptance of creation and the cosmological tenor of the Liturgy. This embodies a worldview that embraces the wholeness of creation, both human and nonhuman. Such an inclusion shows the respect of human beings for the otherness of the rest of creation. This kind of reverence is important in curbing the exploitative culture toward the environment, which is primarily caused by the absence of care and respect to nonhuman others.[78]

Besides emphasizing the holistic worldview embodied in *anaphora* to counter the abusive culture on nature, Zizioulas elaborates on the notion of the priest of creation, regarding it as the new *ethos* of human beings. This provides a crucial link between God and creation, to counter the exploitation of nature. Zizioulas believes that the idea of priest of creation in connection with *anaphora* is a more adequate model to counter the exploitive cultural trend toward nature than the model of steward of creation, which often leads to a utilitarian attitude and behavior toward nonhuman creation.

Zizioulas explicates how a human being, being a link between the Creator God and nature, is the priest of creation who recapitulates creation to God. Since the cosmos was created *ex nihilo* by God, who is absolutely

75. Zizioulas, *Communion and Otherness*, 90.

76. Edwards, "Eucharist and Ecology," 205.

77. Zizioulas, *Eucharistic Communion and World*, 152.

78. Zizioulas, *Communion and Otherness*, 10.

free, recapitulation of creation is ontologically necessary, because whatever is created out of nothing will return to nothingness. Conversely, the created has to depend on and relate to the uncreated God for survival and continuance.[79] The mission of recapitulating creation to God is given to human beings alone because through corporealness, humanity is connected to all creation. Through this material bonding signified by the human body, all creation can enter into communion with God through human beings.[80] Now the church, being the Body of Christ, which acts as the priest of creation, unites the world and refers it back to God, causing it to have communion with him through the Eucharist.[81] When the bishop says the *anaphora* prayer, he invokes the Holy Spirit, *epiclesis*, to transform the gifts of creation and the eucharistic community into the Body of Christ. Therefore, in the Eucharist, the whole creation enters in the trinitarian communion with the eucharistic community. It is a foretaste of the *eschaton*—the transfiguration and recapitulation of the whole creation to God in the end time through the Holy Spirit. After tasting this eschatological flavor of the recapitulation of nature, Zizioulas expects the faithful to go back into the world, carrying this liturgical experience to embrace a thankful and holistic attitude toward nature.[82]

It is imperative to point out that Zizioulas believes that moral conduct is a continuation of this liturgical experience.[83] This experience can liberate humanity from the ambition to rule over nature and raise their awareness that communion with the divine life should include all creation, human and nonhuman.[84] The Eucharist mediates and forms the eucharistic *ethos* through *anaphora* and the priest of creation to the church through the Liturgy. This *ethos* of respecting and embracing nature counters the exploitive and anthropocentric cultural current concerning nature, in which the sacrality of God's creation is neglected. In the Orthodox tradition, the sacrality of creation is upheld in thankfulness and the whole universe is a grand cosmic liturgy celebrated before the Creator. In countering the exploitive culture of creation, Zizioulas attempts to bring this liturgical cosmology and the eucharistic vision of the world into the ordinary daily life of human

---

79. Zizioulas, *Eucharistic Communion and World*, 164.

80. Zizioulas, *Lectures*, 89.

81. Zizioulas, *Eucharistic Communion and World*, 138.

82. Ibid., 125.

83. Ibid., 129.

84. Zizioulas, *Being as Communion*, 120.

beings by explicating that the eucharistic *ethos* of *anaphora* and the priest of creation can be implemented in this present life.[85]

Individualism

Zizioulas claims that the Eucharist is a communion of otherness, from which comes the *ethos* of otherness. He advocates that the meeting and greeting of communion and otherness in the Eucharist helps save humanity from individualistic culture, because in the patristic tradition, the Eucharist is the most anti-individualistic aspect of the church, a true way moving toward and connecting neighbors.[86] Its capacity to be anti-individualistic is based on the communion of the persons in the Trinity as well as the hypostasization in Christ to bring others into communion with the Father God.

In patristic teaching, the Father is the person and sole cause (*monarchia*) of the Trinity. The Father wills the persons of the Son and the Holy Spirit into existence or being, and to have communion with him. This causality is ontological and relational, because it is incomprehensible to speak of the Father without the Son and the Spirit. As such, God is one and three at the same time. The unity or communion of the Trinity is sustained by *monarchia*. Because of the unifying *monarchia*, the primordial communion of the Trinity consists of the three persons who are absolute other to each one. In the primordial communion, the three persons are unique and particular. Put differently, the communion generates otherness and does not threaten it.[87] Therefore, Zizioulas argues that the Eucharist is the ontological affirmation of otherness and uniqueness given by the communion in the Trinity. The *eros* of the Father, which is shared in the Trinity, is now extended to human beings through hypostasization in the Son. This is necessary because they cannot be hypostases without being hypostasized in the one and unique hypostasis of the Son, who is the unique hypostasis of the Father. Zizioulas also states that uniqueness does not exclude other particular beings; it rather affirms their otherness in communion; as he puts it, the Other affirms others.[88] Besides affirming communion, the Eucharist

---

85. Zizioulas, *Eucharistic Communion and World*, 123.

86. Ibid., 128.

87. Zizioulas, *Communion and Otherness*, 5.

88. Ibid.,74.

sanctifies otherness.[89] While the world believes that difference divides, the Eucharist affirms that otherness is *diaphora* but not *diairesis* (difference but not separation).[90] Zizioulas points out that in the Eucharist, difference neither divides nor causes separation; rather, difference is indispensable for communion. Therefore, he argues that if anyone is denied the right to take part in the Eucharist based on any natural or social difference, the validity of the Liturgy is shattered.[91] In other words, the Eucharist cannot co-exist in the spirit and practice of exclusiveness. Zizioulas contests that in this way, the Eucharist is precisely diametrically different from the individualistic cultural current, which always divides and separates the tapestry of relationships, be it with human or nonhuman creation. As such, the Eucharist, as the communion of otherness, is a counter-formation to individualism, which rejects inclusiveness.

In countering individualism, Zizioulas further explicates that the Eucharist is the culmination of communion in which inclusiveness is upheld. It signifies the *ethos* of otherness in that the otherness and uniqueness of others are respected and embraced because of their ontological particularity and integrity conferred by the Father, who is perfectly free. This absolute freedom of the Father God is inseparable from personhood, because personhood is inconceivable without freedom, namely, "the freedom of being other,"[92] which means the freedom to be others or to be yourself. Put differently, personhood means not freedom from others but freedom for others. It is noteworthy that the freedom from other is exclusive and is one of the characteristics of individualism. As Robert Bellah points out, the overwhelming reference, if not the only reference to the self, is a secularized freedom that excludes or is completely free from the concerns of other relationships and institutions.[93] Cultural current can be reckoned as this freedom from others which turns out to be a habit of being utterly self-reliant in terms of attitudes, feelings, and conduct.[94] The individualistic cultural trend causes the protection of one's rights in fear of and against others. This fear of others damages the social fabric and community life. In complete contrast to the exclusiveness of individualism, the freedom for

89. Ibid., 7.

90. Ibid.

91. Ibid.

92. Ibid., 9.

93. Bellah, "Return of Religion," 44.

94. Hopper, *Rebuilding Communities*, 213.

others culminates in the Eucharist. Zizioulas explains that diametrically opposed to individualism, which centers on the self, the *ethos* of otherness in the Eucharist is actually ascetic, because it denies self-love or an exclusive attitude toward others.[95] In fact, it is the *ethos* of giving oneself to others, which is sacrificial and kenotic. Just like Christ, who gave his life sacrificially to all others, those who feast at the Lord's Table also share this self-giving of Christ. While they participate in the Eucharist, they participate in the *ethos* of self-giving. Hence, the Eucharist is a countercultural liturgy against individualistic culture, because the *ethos* of otherness, meaning the self-giving and inclusive attitude toward others, is nurtured and formed by the Eucharist.

THE COUNTERCULTURAL FUNCTION OF THE EUCHARIST ACCORDING TO ZIZIOULAS'S INTERPRETATION

From the above discussion, it is apparent that Zizioulas upholds the countercultural significance of the Eucharist in addressing the exploitive culture of creation and also individualism. He also urges the Orthodox Church to recognize the Eucharist's cultural significance to ordinary people's life. He asserts that "the Orthodox Church must draw more and more from its liturgical life, particularly the Eucharist," which is the recapitulation of the entire world into the discussion of the new cultural current.[96] He elaborates on this assertion from two perspectives. First, the Eucharist must be celebrated properly if it has any significance to offer the world. This aspect has to do with the liturgical experience of the participants, which he believes may make a difference to their way of life. Second, the Eucharist must be interpreted in a way that is relevant and important to humanity's temporal situation.[97] Regarding the celebration and liturgical experience, Zizioulas stresses the imperative significance of the employing of the basic elements from creation and people's ordinary lives in the Eucharist and how they are accepted and lifted up to God, and thus transcended beyond their ordinariness in the communion. In respect of the relevance of the Eucharist to the human situation, Zizioulas draws on the patristic tradition to explain that in this employing and transcending of the elements and the ordinary

95. Zizioulas, *Communion and Otherness*, 81, 84.

96. Zizioulas, *One and Many*, 400.

97. Ibid.

life, culture and history are also accepted, sanctified, and transcended.[98] He explains further that since the Eucharist is relational and thus inevitably incarnational in nature, it must accept culture and history. At the same time, he astutely notes that there is a "prophetic and critical element in the truth as communion."[99] Zizioulas's concept of the prophetic and critical element in the communion can be re-interpreted as something offered by the church, which is different from the culture of the world. In other words, it is something countercultural.

Moreover, the way Zizioulas understands the dialogue between the church and the Greek culture in early church history can illustrate what he means by the prophetic and critical elements in communion. He argues that the early church was cautious of the weaknesses of the Greek culture. The Church Fathers critically assessed the ancient culture and proposed alternatives to it.[100] Thus, he urges the church today to enter into conversation with the prevailing culture in depth, bear a critical attitude against the mainstream culture, and present itself as an alternative to the predominant culture.[101] Being an alternative to mainstream culture, the church can raise its prophetic voice and a critique. This alternative being, or presence of the church, is best embodied not only by *Logos* or our words, but also by a living presence of a Person in the Eucharist.[102] This kind of presence, as Zizioulas means it, resonates with Louis-Marie Chauvet's discussion on sacramental presence, or the way of living, by focusing on the eucharistic presence.[103] For example, the breaking of bread is the eucharistic presence of Christ, namely, *kenosis*, which should be produced in the ecclesial body as a way of life.[104] Both Zizioulas and Chauvet agree that the Eucharist can counter cultural currents that are contrary to Christian identity and values.[105]

To return to Zizioulas, the idea of the living presence of a Person in the Eucharist as an alternative to the prevailing cultural trend explains why he does not believe in legal rules or ethical criteria to counter cultural currents. The challenge must be personal in the sense that it takes the liturgical

98. Zizioulas, *Being as Communion*, 117.

99. Ibid., 118.

100. Zizioulas, *One and Many*, 392–93.

101. Ibid., 393.

102. Zizioulas, *Eucharistic Communion and World*, 129.

103. See Chauvet, "The Broken Bread," 236–62.

104. Ibid., 261.

105. Ibid.

beings that have gone through the transformation of liturgical experience to live out the eucharistic *ethos* inducted by the Eucharist.[106] The eucharistic *ethos* meant by Zizioulas actually refers to a new culture carried by the Eucharist. Its liturgical dimension infuses and nurtures the participants to thoroughly change their attitude to be an alternative to the cultural currents, which run contrary to the mandates of God.

Thus, it is apparent that Zizioulas believes that the Eucharist is of the utmost cultural significance, because it can form attitudes to counter the cultural current without imposing any ethics externally. In his opinion, ethics imposed without a good *ethos* is of little use.[107] Yet, the test of his reason and beliefs lies in the validity of his theological interpretation of the countercultural function of the Eucharist, namely, the eucharistic *ethos* of *anaphora*, the priest of creation, and the eucharistic *ethos* of otherness.

According to Zizioulas, the inadequacy of legal rules and the enforcement of ethics in countering the ecological crisis are apparent. In order to manage the pressing environmental problem, humanity needs a deeper motivation that goes beyond mere legislation and obligations. To fuel this motivation, Zizioulas advocates the concepts of *anaphora* and the priest of creation to formulate the eucharistic *ethos*. He contests that participants who are fueled with the liturgical experience are more motivated to continue this experience in their moral conduct toward the environment.[108] In this way, Zizioulas's proposal of the exploitive culture on nature is quite theologically valid through *anaphora* and the priest of creation of the Eucharist, through which creation is on the journey of becoming perfect. Still, a theological explanation is needed to elucidate and concretize how an *ethos*, or more concretely "an operational set of attitudes and values" can arise from the Eucharist to counter a tremendously escalating ecological abuse.[109] Some scholars, like Andrew Shepherd, argues for Zizioulas that the *ethos* raised by him would stop ecological activism at the outset and invite the expression of gratitude for the giveness of nature, which can be embodied in the Sabbath, prayers and meditation.[110] Though such a comment sounds as ascetic as Zizioulas may want eucharistic *ethos* to be, one may have doubts about the passivity in this kind of experience and how

---

106. Zizioulas, *Eucharistic Communion and World*, 141, 145.

107. Ibid., 141.

108. Ibid., 129.

109. Keightley, "Church's Laity," 319.

110. Shepherd, "Other," 6–7.

it may have adequate stamina to effectively address environmental issues. In light of the increasing severity of the ecological problems plaguing the world now, it is reasonable for the church to hope for and seek a more active approach that is also valid theologically. How would this rather receptive and thanksgiving aspect of Zizioulas's eucharistic *ethos* be more theologically concrete and more effective in countering ecological abuse? It could have been more celebrated if Zizioulas had discussed how the eucharistic *ethos* regarding nature can be nurtured and translated into attitudes and actions operative in addressing the exploitive culture of creation.

Zizioulas proposes to counter individualism through the *ethos* of otherness embodied by the Eucharist, because in the Orthodox tradition the Liturgy is the most anti-individualistic act of the ecclesial community.[111] The Eucharist as a communion of otherness mirrors the *taxis* of the Trinity, which is asymmetrical and held together by the Father who is *monarchia*, the one cause. Likewise, the hierarchy of the church is asymmetrical. Both the Eucharist and the church are presided over by the bishop, who vivifies the asymmetry of *monarchia*. Zizioulas argues that unlike the usual derogatory sense associated with the asymmetric hierarchy, *monarchia* is not an impasse to communion, because the Father is absolutely free to will the existence of the Son and the Spirit. This absolute freedom is the basis of freedom for otherness, which is imperative to curb individualism. Thus, celebration of the Eucharist is the upholding and living of this freedom for others and also the nurturing of an attitude for otherness.

However, Zizioulas's proposal is subject to doubts. He defends the *monarchia* Father as the cause and sustainer of communion between the persons in the Trinity. *Monarchia* also establishes the foundation of communion of otherness in the Eucharist and the church. Yet, it is precisely his defense of *monarchia* that causes skeptics to query the validity of his interpretation of the Eucharist to counter individualism and also his rationale for the asymmetrical structure of the Eucharist and the church. This is because this asymmetry in the Trinity, the Eucharist, and the church is not conducive to reciprocity, which is important to resist individualistic culture.

A former student of Zizioulas, Nicholaos Loudovikos's argument can help us understand how Zizioulas's asymmetrical account of the Trinity actually impedes the validity of his interpretation of the Eucharist in addressing individualism. He critically challenges two major features,

---

111. Zizioulas, *Eucharistic Communion and World*, 128.

namely, the repulsion of ousianic character and the rejection of reciprocity in Zizioulas's account of *monarchia,* both of which are crucial in his proposal for constituting and maintaining the communion of otherness in the Eucharist.[112] It is true that Zizioulas argues that the Nicene-Constantinopolitan Creed changed the Creed of Nicaea in the Council of Constantinople (381 CE). The change was the switch from "the generation of the Son 'from the substance of the Father'" to "the Son was born simply 'from the Father.'"[113]Zizioulas regards this change as a confirmation of the Fathers' resistance to a substantialist account of the unity of God. Accordingly, he takes this switch in the patristic tradition and makes it almost a rejection of substance in the origin and maintenance of the unity of the Trinity. However, Loudovikos urges a re-reading of Gregory Nazianzen (whom Zizioulas emphasizes because he presided over the Council of Constantinople) on this subject. Loudovikos references Gregory Nazianzen; that monarchy cannot be restricted to one person because it takes plurality for unity to come into existence. Such unity is brought by both equality of nature, and convergence of agreed opinion and motion of the persons of equal nature. In this way, though the Trinity is numerically distinct, *ousia* remains undivided.[114] Loudovikos argues that according to Gregory Nazianzen, both the substantialist and the personalist accounts of the monarchy can co-exist. The unity is not limited to one person, the Father, and there is an equality of nature in which the two converge into one. Loudovikos further explicates Gregory's idea that the unity of God is a "complete consubstantiality and convergence of the persons" resulting in a "reciprocal self-offering" which differentiates the uncreated and the created.[115]

It is obvious that Loudovikos's reading of Gregory is very different from that of Zizioulas, which is personalist—without reciprocity as far as Loudovikos is concerned. The challenge to Zizioulas is whether his account of *monarchia* of the Father truly allows mutual self-offering. Zizioulas insists that the Father is *monarchia,* the only one who is active in constituting the Son and the Spirit, while the Son and the Spirit only condition or confirm the Father. He maintains that this *monarchia* is an asymmetry in order. He defends this asymmetry as ontological rather than moral or functional. However, there is no principle mandating that the cause is greater than the

112. Loudovikos, "Person instead of Grace," 689.

113. Zizioulas, *Communion and Otherness,* 120.

114. Loudovikos, "Person instead of Grace," 691.

115. Ibid.

effect and the one who wills to love first is higher than those who are being loved. Love, after all, is reciprocal in nature. In fact, an asymmetrical relationship can dampen, if not inhibit full reciprocal love or self-offering. This is because along an asymmetry, relationship is more one-dimensional in the sense that otherness is given or dictated (using Loudovikos's term) from the high end of the asymmetry to the low one.[116] Therefore, Loudovikos rightly observes and criticizes that Zizioulas's asymmetrical *monarchia* risks the imposition of dictated otherness, which makes others passive and thus deters reciprocal otherness, or self-offering. A more accurate question would be: is dictated otherness not otherness for others at all if they are not free to return their otherness? Since otherness should be reciprocal, it is doubtful whether the dictated otherness can really confer communion of otherness. In fact, dictated otherness can stand a good chance of making the relationship inevitably totalitarian, warns Loudovikos.[117] Since the mutual self-offering of the asymmetrical hierarchy in the Trinity is questionable, Zizioulas's account of the *ethos* of otherness in the Eucharist, which is based on the communion of the Trinity, is not as valid as he intends it in countering individualism. This is because the individualistic culture is basically sheer self-love, which discourages self-giving.

Besides his challenges to Zizioulas's account of *monarchia* and its impact on the trinitarian theology and otherness, Loudovikos also questions its impact on the ecclesial body, which is supposedly crucial for de-individualization in the Orthodox tradition. In particular, he is concerned with the impact of the asymmetrical structure of the Trinity on Christology and the church, because it affects how Christ relates to his Body. First, Loudovikos cautions that care must be exercised in drawing "parallels between the Trinity, christology, and the Church."[118] On the one hand since God is God who created all beings, truth, and meaning, it is possible that the created share some relatedness to him, including how the structure of the triune God is applicable to or reflected by the world.[119] On the other hand, the relationship between the Father and the other two persons is not identical with the relationship between Christ and his members. The order of the-one-and-the-many in the Trinity is not quite the same as that in the

116. Loudovikos, *Eucharistic Ontology*, 10.

117. Loudovikos, "Person instead of Grace," 694.

118. See Loudovikos, "Christian Life," 131.

119. Gunton, *One, Three, and Many*, 149–50.

church,[120] because the relationship among the uncreated is qualitatively different from the relationship between the uncreated and the created.[121] Because of this qualitative difference, any particular application of the trinitarian transcendental should not be a blanket transfer. It should need further considerations at different levels and be open to analogical exploration or qualification, as suggested by Collin Gunton.[122] Second, though it is true that the church (so also the Eucharist) is the icon of the Kingdom of God, it should be taken as an "apophatic icon" but not a transcendental one imposed as an automatic institutional reflection of the Kingdom of God above history.[123] In the same vein Volf denounces Zizioulas for paying no heed to the dialectic of "ready—not yet" in this over-realization of *eschaton*.[124] In particular, he questions the bipolarity between the group of bishop, presbyters and deacons and the group of laity, which puts the bishop in an even more superior position to the laity. Then, it is doubtful whether the church, which is supposed to be a place for communion of reciprocal otherness, can be effective in curbing individualism, as Zizioulas proposes and envisages. If this bipolarity is taken to an extreme, the risk is the emergence of totalitarianism, a caution already signaled by Loudovikos.

Given the asymmetrical interpretation of *monarchia* by Zizioulas, his proposal of the Eucharist as *ethos* of otherness to counter individualism is subject to reasonable doubt—can reciprocity be truly permissible within an asymmetrical relationship, without any possibility of some kind of dictated otherness? This suspicion is leveled not only against the Eucharist *per se* but also the church structure. Thus, the validity of Zizioulas's proposal to counter the individualistic culture through the *ethos* of otherness in the Eucharist, which is based on the asymmetrical Trinity, is questionable.

SUMMARY

This chapter has examined how the trinitarian doctrine in the patristic tradition has impacted Zizioulas's interpretation of the Eucharist and the ecclesiology. The ecclesiological implications of the Eucharist reflect Zizioulas's idea of how the Trinity doctrine has prescribed the structure of the

120. See Loudovikos, "Christian Life," 130.

121. Volf, *After Our Likeness*, 211.

122. Gunton, *One, Three, and Many*, 166–67, 170.

123. See Loudovikos, "Christian Life," 131.

124. Volf, *After Our Likeness*, 101.

Liturgy and the church. Moreover, his cosmological interpretation of the Eucharist connects the Eucharist to the material world, rendering the Liturgy as the acceptance and affirmation of nature. Such acceptance and affirmation of creation in the Eucharist is naturally contrary to the prevailing ecological abuse around the world. Zizioulas further draws on St. Maximus the Confessor's concept of priest of creation to address the exploitive nature of culture on creation by highlighting that in the Eucharist, the church acts as the priest of creation to recapitulate nature. He relies on the liturgical experience gone through by the participants to shape the eucharistic *ethos,* which helps counter environmental problems. Though his interpretation of the Eucharist regarding ecological abuse is theologically valid, questions such as how an operational set of attitudes and values can be inculcated should demand more consideration.

Besides the abusive nature of culture on creation, Zizioulas alerts us to the sprawling individualism. He proposes that in the Orthodox tradition, the Eucharist is the most anti-individualistic act of the church. He reasons that from the one-and-the-many in the Eucharist, which reflects the unity and plurality in the Trinity initiated and sustained by *monarchia,* flows the *ethos* of otherness, which is actually freedom for others. Zizioulas argues that such freedom for others counteracts individualism, which is actually a culture obsessed by freedom from others. However, Zizioulas has to face challenges raised against *monarchia,* because it makes the relationship among the three persons in the Trinity asymmetrical. This asymmetry causes doubts about full reciprocity in the Trinity. Since in Zizioulas's ecclesiology the Trinity is the basis of the Eucharist, it is reasonable to query the validity of interpreting the Eucharist as the most anti-individualistic act against individualism, as he claims.

5

Miroslav Volf's Interpretation of the Eucharist

Countering the Culture of Social Exclusion

INTRODUCTION

MIROSLAV VOLF (1956–) was born in Osijek, Croatia when it was still part of the Socialist Federal Republic of Yugoslavia. The society into which he was born was primarily Roman Catholic. In his early childhood, his family moved to Novi Sad in Serbia, which was a multicultural city where the main faith was the Orthodox Church. Volf and his family lived as a minority in both towns because of their Protestant background. His experience of living in different church neighborhoods and multicultural backgrounds explains his orientation toward engaging in ecumenical and cultural dialogues in his theological career. For example, his first postdoctoral publication, *After Our Likeness,* exemplifies his keen interest in ecumenical dialogue concerning trinitarian doctrine. This is where he engages with Joseph Ratzinger and John Zizioulas.[1] As a Croatian Protestant who had lived at the margin of European society in his early years, Volf was well aware of the gravity of cultural clashes and ethnic cleansings that have taken place around the world, especially in Europe. The fact that he is the founding Director of the

1. Volf, *After Our Likeness,* 24.

Yale Center for Faith and Culture also reflects his passion and competence in dialogue between faiths and cultures for the good of humanity. His experience in ecumenical dialogues, endeavors in understanding the complexity between faiths and cultures, and also his comparative study on Zizioulas and Ratzingar, who come from the Orthodox and the Catholic tradition respectively, explain why Volf is included in this interdisciplinary and cross-church tradition research on the Eucharist's countercultural function.

In this chapter, the doctrine of the Trinity will be examined together with Volf's ecclesiology to evaluate the position and significance of the Eucharist in his system. The second part of this chapter focuses on what he identifies as the most dreadful cultural current, namely, social exclusion due to "non-recognition or misrecognition" of cultural identities.[2] The third part investigates how Volf draws upon Protestant theology to show ways in which the Eucharist can be countercultural to exclusive culture. Finally, the validity of the way Volf addresses this cultural current through the Eucharist is assessed.

VOLF'S INTERPRETATION OF THE EUCHARIST

Among Volf's publications, *After Our Likeness* is a relatively detailed and systematic delineation of his doctrine of the Trinity and the church. It is important to note that he wrote this book with the purpose of criticizing the "pyramidal" ecclesiology of Ratzinger and the "bipolarity" of the ecclesial community of Zizioulas. One of its main purposes is to suggest a church model of "polycentric and symmetrical reciprocity of the many,"[3] which is characterized by mutuality of the church members. Being well aware of the possible queries of these hierarchical ecclesiologies and individualism in Free Church ecclesiology, Volf proposes a non-individualistic and nonhierarchical ecclesiology rooted in an egalitarian doctrine of the Trinity for the Free Church. Under the framework of Volf's doctrine of the Trinity, which gives the basis of ecclesiology, the position and significance of the Eucharist will be reviewed.

---

2. Volf, *Exclusion and Embrace*, 19.

3. Volf, *After Our Likeness*, 217.

The Correspondences between the Trinity and the Church

The subtitle of *After Our Likeness, The Church as the Image of the Trinity* suggests that Volf considers that certain correspondences between the Trinity and the church exist. He presents the subtlety of such correspondence, which is subject to limits and qualifications, rather than just being a blanket transfer from the Trinity to the church.[4] On one hand, Volf explains that human beings can only worship, but cannot imitate, God's mysterious triune nature. He does not mean to negate the spirituality of the imitation of Christ. Rather, he means that the full reciprocal interiority of the divine persons cannot be imitated completely by human beings. On the other hand, the indwelling of the triune God in history and the world makes the connection between God and the church, which is the indwelling place of God, more than a possibility, and possibly a necessity.[5] It seems clear that Volf focuses more on the economic Trinity than the immanent Trinity; he is more concerned with the engagement of God in the world through the church. Given his emphasis on the economic Trinity, queries about his understanding of the relationship between the immanent Trinity and the economic Trinity may arise. For example, both Kevin J. Bidwell and A. James Reimer question if Volf has made adequate differentiation between the immanent Trinity and the economic Trinity.[6] However, Volf defends his awareness of such a distinction and defends himself against the criticism. In claiming the correspondence between the Trinity and the church, Volf explains that he focuses on the economic Trinity in building the connection between the Trinity and the church without neglecting the immanent Trinity.[7]

Volf suggests that one major reflection of the correspondences between the triune God and the church is the relationship between the one and the many. God alone is the basis of "both unity and multiplicity" for God is a communion of the divine persons.[8] The correspondence of the Trinity's communion of one and the many is realized in the Christian initiation, baptism. In baptism, believers are welcomed and received into the ecclesial communion, vivifying the unity in multiplicity in the name of the

4. See Volf, "Being as God Is," 4–5.

5. Volf, *After Our Likeness*, 192.

6. Bidwell, *Church as Image*, 201; Reimer, "Miroslav Volf," 14.

7. Volf, "Trinity is Our Social Program," 407.

8. Volf, *After Our Likeness*, 193.

Father, the Son, and the Holy Spirit. The initiation process is a "simultaneous incorporation into both trinitarian and ecclesial communion."[9] This unity in church multiplicity mirrors the mutual loving communion of the Trinity. As such, the ecclesial communion exemplifies and shares God's triune nature in the Christian initiation and ecclesial life. In this way, the church corresponds to and reflects the Trinity. Volf further argues that since its early inception, the church has had a growing consciousness of the activity of the Father, the Son and the Holy Spirit in salvation history.[10]

With respect to the limits of the correspondences, Volf maintains that it is not a straight forward transfer from the Trinity to the church, because human beings are creations of the triune God, and they can only correspond to God analogously and creaturely.[11] This is because the person and communion in the doctrine of Trinity have no exact equivalents in ecclesiology. There is a decreasing extent of correspondence of communion between the divine persons, between God and the church, and between human beings intra-ecclesially, and finally between churches.[12] Volf explicates the tension of correspondence and limits of the Trinity *vis-à-vis* the church before elucidating the crux of his doctrine of the Trinity, the perichoretic Trinity, which has significant implications for ecclesiology and also the Eucharist.

Perichoretic Trinity and the Church

Much influenced by Jürgen Moltmann, Volf proposes the perichoretic personhood of the divine persons in the Trinity to support the foundation of the church, and gives the theological ground of nonhierarchical ecclesiology for the Free Church. Volf contests that the divine persons are real subjects capable of action; they are not purely relations. Person and relation emerge concurrently and mutually constitute one another.[13] This idea is influenced by Moltmann's doctrine of the Trinity: "Here there are no persons without relations; but there are no relations without persons either. Person and relation are complementary."[14] Volf highlights that in this complementary relationship, the divine persons constitute each other

9. Ibid., 197.
10. Ibid., 195.
11. Ibid., 199.
12. Ibid., 211.
13. Ibid., 205.
14. Moltmann, *Trinity and Kingdom*, 172.

mutually, and they are inconceivable without these relations. Through mutual giving and receiving, their own divine personhood maintains its own uniqueness while they affirm other persons.[15] Hence, there is full reciprocity in the Trinity.

Volf adopts the term *perichoresis* to express the reciprocal interiority of the trinitarian persons. *Perichoresis* is the "self-donation" of the divine persons to one another.[16] The divine persons are mutually internal to each other, as revealed by Jesus: "so that you may know and understand that the Father is in me and I am in the Father."[17] In addition to their mutual constitution, the divine persons are giving and receiving. The perichoretic divine persons are interpenetrating each other without demolishing their own particularity and the trinitarian plurality.[18]

Volf relates catholicity and unity to perichoretic personhood. He calls the "reciprocal interiority" of the divine persons their catholicity because each divine person carries other persons within itself.[19] Due to the complete openness toward other divine persons, the divine persons are completely catholic. Volf suggests that the catholicity of the divine persons constitutes the unity of the Trinity without relying on the numeric oneness,[20] that is, the one substance or the *monarchia* of the Father. The former risks the challenge of being a-personal and the latter asymmetrical. Volf maintains that mutual love in the trinitarian communion forms the basis of the non-individualistic and nonhierarchical ecclesiology. He proposes such an egalitarian church model to the Free Church.

As previously mentioned, the incorporation into the ecclesial communion is trinitarian. Both the doctrine of the Trinity and the ecclesial body are perichoretic. The communion of the ecclesial members reflects the trinitarian unity, meaning they embody the reciprocal love of the divine persons.[21] Yet, Volf points out that this correspondence between the perichoretic Trinity and the church is subject to limits. The trinitarian *perichoresis* finds its correspondences in different degrees at both the ecclesial level and the inter-ecclesial level.

---

15. Volf, *After Our Likeness*, 205.

16. Volf, "Trinity is Our Social Program," 412.

17. John 10:38; 14:10–11; 17:21.

18. Volf, "Trinity is Our Social Program," 409.

19. Volf, *After Our Likeness*, 209.

20. Ibid., 210.

21. Ibid., 195.

First of all, while the interiority of the divine persons is completely re-ciprocal, this is not the case between God and human beings. Volf explains that the "personal interiority is one-sided" as far as the relation between God and human beings is concerned.[22] Therefore, the Holy Spirit, as the subject, can indwell a human being but not *vice versa*. However, he explains that this asymmetry does not deter the mutual love between God and hu-man beings because the human being can be a loving self, a self that can embrace the other without indwelling that other: while the Father and the Son through the Holy Spirit indwell human beings, human beings indwell the *"life-giving ambience of the Spirit"* (emphasis original).[23] This is the way that the reciprocity between God and human beings corresponds to *perichoresis*.

Volf further explicates that at the ecclesial level, "only the *interiority of personal characteristics* (emphasis original) can correspond to the in-teriority of the divine persons."[24] Put simply, there is no overlapping of subjectivities among human beings who, however, can mutually influence each other's lives through the inter-flowing of personal characteristics. This explains why Volf maintains that faith is mediated ecclesially, because learning the language of faith takes place in "ecclesial socialization" in the congregation.[25] Volf states emphatically that the Holy Spirit indwells hu-man beings and opens them for this inter-flowing, thus causing them to become catholic persons. This is how the catholicity of Christians corre-sponds to that of the divine persons. Volf also underscores that the catholic-ity of the church members is inseparable from the catholicity of the church. Christians are catholic because of the indwelling of Christ inasmuch as the church is catholic because Christ indwells it through the Holy Spirit.[26]

Volf maintains that at the inter-ecclesial level, *perichoresis* of the Trin-ity cannot be the basis for inter-ecclesial unity, because if human beings cannot be internal to each other, it is even less likely that churches can be internal to one another. Volf does not expound much on the catholicity at the inter-ecclesial level, though he believes that the issue of "the minimum of catholicity is of crucial importance in ecumenical relations."[27] Volf is

22. Ibid., 211.
23. Ibid.
24. Ibid.
25. Ibid., 163.
26. Ibid., 278.
27. Ibid., 269.

neither particularly meticulous about catholicity at the inter-ecclesial level, nor does he think that the relationship between the universal church and local churches is necessary. While acknowledging that a local church cannot stand alone in order to be catholic, but has to be connected with an ecclesiological whole which transcends itself, Volf argues that the transcending ecclesiological whole should be the eschatological gathering of God's people, but not the universal church. That Volf is content with a "to-be-realized" eschatology rather than a universal church has a great impact on his ecclesiology. His future oriented eschatology actually impedes his effort in emphasizing the catholicity of local churches in this present age. Avery Dulles astutely criticizes Volf on this point: given Volf's "futurist" eschatology, for the present it is not necessary for the local churches to be in actual communion with each other in this world.[28] Volf's undermining of an existing universal church may make the local churches more equal and complete on their own. However, it also makes the local churches more individualistic, a characteristic for which the Free Church has long been criticized.

This outline of the doctrine of perichoretic Trinity and the correspondence of the Trinity and the church shows that Volf proposes to construct a trinitarian doctrine which is a more symmetrical reciprocity, in order to support an egalitarian ecclesiology. This would mean equality among individual members as well as the churches. This egalitarian church model is also polycentric-participative in that Christians serve one another through mutual giving and receiving of gifts bestowed by the Spirit.[29] Volf further spells out the ecclesiality of the church, which is basically identified as an assembly confessing the faith by word and sacraments.

Ecclesiality of the Church

Volf explains ecclesiality in terms of the identity as well as the identification of the church. The identity of the church is established on its future—it is the mutual or reciprocal personal indwelling of the triune God and his gathered people in God's new creation. In other words, it is the eschatological fulfillment of the perfect communion of believers with the triune God.[30] Yet this perfect future communion has its concrete experiences and

28. Dulles, Review of *After Our Likeness,* 51.

29. Volf, *After Our Likeness,* 227.

30. Ibid., 128.

perceivable expressions in the present time. These present experiences and expressions help identification of the church, which is certainly inseparable from the church's identity.[31]

Volf identifies the church as a gathering of believers in the name of Christ in a specific place for worshipping God and ecclesially mediating faith. He subscribes to the definition proposed by the First Baptist, John Smyth's (c. 1570–1612),[32] a strong allusion to the book of Matthew 20:18, which forms the basis of Smyth's congregational ecclesiology of the Free Church. This stipulates that the church is a visible communion of saints bounded by covenant with God and themselves.[33] Given the scope of this chapter, suffice it to say that Volf regards one of the identifications of the church is a concrete assembly of believers in a specific locale for communally worshipping God and instructing the believers.

Naturally, questions concerning the relationship between the local church and the universal church are raised. As previously mentioned, Volf maintains that the local church is the anticipation of the gathered people of God in the *eschaton*. It is not a concrete, existing universal church. The universal church, at its best, is more like a summation of all the local churches.[34] For Volf, each local church is catholic, though it is only part of the universal church. He further explains this point as being through the Holy Spirit, Christ present in Christians, and in local churches, that also connect to each other through the Spirit in Christ. In this way, the local church is catholic as it is connected to the universal church.[35] Yet questions about how such catholicity of the local church and its connection to other local churches are expressed demands further explanation from Volf.

Volf is well aware of the charges against the early Free Church being too subjective and individualistic, and thus causing it to fail to be *de facto* catholic. He is also aware of the objective dimension of the ecclesiality of the Catholic Church and the Orthodox Church[36] In order to allay these charges Volf underscores the identification of the local church through confession by word and sacraments, in accordance with Smyth's commu-

31. Ibid., 129.

32. The title of the First Baptist is given to John Smyth because he is generally recognized as the first Baptist minister of the first Baptist Church in modern times.

33. Ibid., 135.

34. Ibid., 140–41.

35. Ibid., 145.

36. Ibid., 134.

nion ecclesiology. The confession in ecclesial communion counters the charge that in the early Free Church the benefits of salvation were mediated by "pious feelings or individual faith."[37]

Volf further explains that through confession both the "cognitive specification and personal identification coincided."[38] The former refers to who Jesus Christ is, while the latter is the commitment of the individual, pledged by confessing the cognitive content. However, confession is not merely cognitive, because it has to be performed in order to be a confession. Confession is also commitment, because the one who confesses commits oneself to what is confessed.[39] Thus, confession is by no means purely cognitive, or private, or individualistic. It is precisely because it is communal and perceivable that it helps identify a church. Volf expects that in the confession of a Christian assembly the objective and the subjective conditions of ecclesiality meet. Moreover, according to Volf's understanding, the confession, which is a constituting mark of the church, should be "pluriform" or multi-dimensional compared to the "'narrow portals' of *ordained office* (emphasis original)."[40]

The idea of the pluriform of confession explains that in Volf's ecclesiology, the confession of faith is not just the word but also the sacraments. Unlike those who subscribe to the Zwinglian sacramental theology and are suspicious of the dissociation of grace from personal faith in those sacramental theories,[41] he connects the association of the sacraments and personal faith by drawing upon Luther's principle that "if you believe, you have it; if you do not believe, you do not have it."[42]

The purpose of Volf's insistence on the multi-dimensional confession as a constituting mark of the church is to resist the domineering impact of identification of the church by the ordained office. In stark contrast to the Catholic and Orthodox traditions, Volf regards the ordained office as not belonging to *esse*, but to *bene esse* of the church. He does not mean to undermine the service of proclaiming God's word, but rather argues that proclamation should be understood as one of the dimensions of communal

37. Freeman, "Gathered," 263.

38. Volf, *After Our Likeness*, 148.

39. Ibid., 149.

40. Ibid., 152.

41. Freeman, "Gathered," 264.

42. Volf, *After Our Likeness*, 153.

confession of faith.[43] Volf's claim that the ordained office belongs to *bene esse* of the church also leads to his understanding of church structure. This understanding is charismatic and polycentric-participative, fitting his non-hierarchical ecclesiology based on the perichoretic doctrine of the Trinity.

Volf recognizes that church structures are the products of the institutionalization of the church for promoting stable social interaction for the sake of the ecclesial mediation of the faith. However, he contests that church structures should not be objectified and absolutized, because above all, the church is the work of the Holy Spirit. The Spirit bestows *charismata* on Christians according to his discretion. Christians receive *charismata* to serve one another for mutual edification as well as the glorification of God. Moreover, the ministries, which are based on the charismata, are provisional inasmuch as the distribution of charismata is provisional.[44] Because of the provisional nature of the gifts, ordained office is of *bene esse* of the church. Furthermore, the bestowing of gifts by the Spirit makes the church charismatic and polycentric-participative, which is in sharp contrast to the episcopal-centric or hierarchical ecclesial communities. Dulles rightly comments that Volf's polycentric-participative church model draws attention to the passivity of laity in those hierarchical churches.[45]

While the ordained office is *bene esse*, the sacraments of baptism and the Eucharist are of *esse* to the church. Volf argues for this position because throughout church history congregations unceasingly performed baptism and celebrated the Eucharist. "Being a Christian means being baptized and participating in the celebration of the Lord's Supper."[46] Volf regards baptism and the Eucharist as constitutive of the church insofar as they are received with faith and confession. This is characteristic of how Volf superimposes both the objective and subjective dimensions on the ecclesiality of the sacraments, namely, baptism and the Eucharist. Furthermore, Volf suggests that the sacraments embody the crux of Christian beliefs inscribed in them and they enact normative ways for Christian practices or a ritualistic way of life.[47]

From this outline of Volf's ecclesiology of the Free Church, it is not difficult to see his attempts to avoid both the hierarchical ecclesiology and

43. Ibid., 152.
44. Ibid., 244.
45. Dulles, Review of *After Our Likeness*, 52.
46. Volf, *After Our Likeness*, 152.
47. Volf, "Way of Life," 127.

the church structure of the Catholic and Orthodox traditions. He finds it feasible to construct a proposal for a more egalitarian church model based on the perichoretic doctrine of the Trinity. However, the book *After Our Likeness*, in which Volf advocates the idea of *perichoresis* in a more comprehensive way than his other works, does not systematically state his doctrine of the Trinity with sufficient substantiation. Perhaps it is due to the fact that at the outset he subscribes to the idea that "today, the thesis that ecclesial communion should correspond to trinitarian communion enjoys the status of an almost self-evident proposition."[48] Furthermore, his goal in formulating an ecclesiology different from that of Zizioulas and Ratzinger has made him quite selective in presenting his material and reasons against hierarchical ecclesiology without first systematically delineating his doctrine of the Trinity.

In brief, it is just to say that Volf's ecclesiology is not characteristically eucharistic. This is understandable because he is constructing an ecclesiology of the Free Church, in which the church is typically not built on the sacraments. The Word of God seems to receive more attention than the Eucharist. It would not be an exaggeration to say that many free churches lean more toward the memorialism or "Symbolists" of the Zwinglian camp,[49] and regard the Eucharist as a matter of individual piety. Since Volf's task is to construct an ecclesiology of the Free Church, it is understandable that the Eucharist is far more removed from the center of Protestant ecclesiology than in that of the Catholic or the Orthodox Church. Yet, the way Volf understands and presents the Eucharist as *esse* of the church and its relation to the ecclesially mediated faith can potentially revitalize the Eucharist in the Free Church. For example, the Eucharist is more than private piety in Volf's interpretation and in the Eucharist—the objective dimension of a public ritual and the subjective dimension of personal faith overlap. Volf also re-envisions the Eucharist for the Free Church as this: Christians can receive spiritual sustenance through the objective performance of the Eucharist while holding onto the position of personal faith. It is also noteworthy that Volf interprets the Eucharist as the prescription of normative patterns for Christian practice. As such, the Eucharist is a practice-shaping sacrament for Christian lifestyles, which are distinctive from the secular way of life.[50]

48. Volf, *After Our Likeness*, 191.

49. Smith, *To Take Place*, 100.

50. Volf, "Way of Life," 127–28, 131.

VOLF'S ANALYSIS OF THE CULTURE OF SOCIAL EXCLUSION

Definition and Causes of Social Exclusion

Volf identifies the exclusive culture not just in terms of ethnicity, even though he is immensely influenced by ethnic genocides because of his Croatian background. Social exclusion is the rejection of some social groups that are within the boundary of the larger society as a whole. Volf emphasizes "exclusion from a situated *self* (emphasis original), without which exclusions from communities would be unthinkable."[51] Such a self is situated by its cultural captivity and even blindness to its own self-righteousness.[52] This captivity and blindness can, in the name of civilization, often be barbaric. For example, under the disguise of civilization, the European culture of the elite subjugated that of ethnic groups, forcing them to become homogenized into the dominant culture. Volf astutely identifies social exclusion as the flip side of the history of inclusion.[53] In the name of civilization, exclusion has actually become a "crime against the other right."[54] Put differently, social exclusion is an offense against human beings.[55]

Moreover, this offense of exclusion has escalated due to globalization. Globalization has caused rapid population growth, exploitation of resources and migrants, to name just a few of the disturbing repercussions impeding the relationships between different social groups. Volf particularly points out globalization has accelerated conflicts around incompatible visions of social life.[56] Volf further highlights that there are different boundaries existing among the different social groups.[57] These boundaries are now more easily crossed than ever because of globalization, which brings different peoples or the other into contact more frequently and intensively than ever.[58] Those who are fearful of the other may feel more insecure and uncertain toward one and other. As a result, social exclusion may occur in order to eradicate the other for the sake of assuring one's own security.

51. Volf, *Exclusion and Embrace*, 57.

52. Volf, "Vision of Embrace," 197.

53. Volf, *Exclusion and Embrace*, 58–59.

54. Ibid., 60.

55. Jacques, "Confronting the Challenge," 328.

56. Volf, *Flourishing*, 197.

57. Volf, "Vision of Embrace," 196.

58. Sahin and Altuntas, "Enlightened Exclusion," 27.

Volf also points out that the contemporary clashes between different social groups are understood more aptly as conflicts of cultural identity rather than as differences in ideology.[59] He gives a cultural analysis of exclusion. First, consider the strongholds of "symbolic cultural maps," boundaries, and identities.[60] People exclude each other because they are anxious to ward off anything that shakes their own symbolic cultural maps and transgresses accepted boundaries or shatters their identities. Eradication of the other is necessary for restoring the sense of order in one's own world. Second is the human being's desperate desire for "hegemonic centrality."[61] Exclusion happens when people want to be at the center and gain the upper hand to control everything, not to mention the desire to have what others possess.[62] Third is the will to purity. The will to purity is actually a violent re-arrangement of the social worlds, including one's inner world and the external world of all his or her connections.[63] It is violent in the sense that it can be totalitarian at the expense of others' existence by means of elimination, assimilation, domination, and abandonment.[64] It is not an exaggeration to say that the will to purity is tantamount to the sin of purity when the pursuit of it is shifted away from the spiritual life of oneself to the cultural world of the other.[65] This pursuit of purity can be dangerous because it can destroy the totality of a human being or even a social group. Moreover, this sin of purity is not only committed against the person or the social group afflicted by means of exclusion, but also against God. This is because the exclusion of other is the exclusion of God.[66] Volf argues that when the inextricably reciprocal relationship among human beings purported by the Creator God is ruptured by social exclusion, God is violated.[67]

Volf makes two points concerning the relation of Christians and churches to this cultural current. First, he claims that Christianity can cause conflicts leading to social exclusion when Christianity is upheld as

59. Volf, "Vision of Embrace," 196.

60. Volf, *Exclusion and Embrace*, 78.

61. Ibid., 79.

62. Volf, "Vision of Embrace," 201.

63. Volf, *Exclusion and Embrace*, 74.

64. Ibid., 67.

65. Ibid., 74.

66. Volf, "Theological Reflections," 278.

67. Volf, *Exclusion and Embrace*, 65–66.

a cultural badge of a group's identity,[68] and in the name of this marker the Christian group rejects another group. This self-perception of such a marker can jeopardize relations with the other if Christian communities overlook the many players in the larger society and decline to promote the common good of these players.[69] Second, Volf suggests another possibility of causing social exclusion: when a Christian's faith is only superficial, rather than having been nurtured to become ambassadors of peace, there may be a chance that they will become violent aggressors.[70]

Theological Reflections on the Relationships of Culture, Church, and Agency

First, Volf reminds the church to be aware of the fact that her challenge is how to live with the other in the midst of increasing contacts and even conflicts in a diverse cultural setting. Plurality of cultures is a social reality; it is a given. In our close proximity there is always "neighborly other."[71] Volf appeals to church history to explain that since the birth of the Christian church, otherness has been part and parcel of Christian ethnic and cultural identity.[72] Christians identified and understood themselves as aliens toward the end of the New Testament period.[73] This Christian outlook on life is different from the world. However, Volf is not advocating a wholesale rejection of or alienation from the cultures into which the Christians were originally born. He suggests a notion of dialectical "distance and belonging"[74] or a "soft difference"[75] that helps the church respectfully take note of the multiple cultures in the world.

By distance and belonging Volf maintains that a "proper distance from a culture *does not take Christians out of that culture*" (emphasis original).[76] Volf acknowledges that Christians should distance themselves from their own culture due to their ultimate loyalty to God as well as his future world,

68. Volf, "Grave," 7.

69. Volf, *Public Faith*, 79.

70. Volf, "Grave," 7.

71. Volf, "Living," 11.

72. Volf, "Theological Reflections," 270.

73. 1 Pet 2:11.

74. Volf, "Vision of Embrace," 197.

75. Volf, "Soft Difference," 15.

76. Volf, "Vision of Embrace," 198.

in which people of all nations and all cultures will gather. However, it is imperative to recognize that distancing oneself without belonging isolates, and belonging without distance destroys. Therefore, Volf believes that both distance and belonging are equally important to the formation of Christian identity. He further explains that although Christians have distanced themselves from their old cultures, the body of Christ encompasses all cultures.[77] Therefore, Christians can still find that they belong to culture. Volf concludes that the cultural identity of Christians is formed by the "interpenetration" of their distance and belonging regarding the cultures they are from or in.[78]

Furthermore, the interpenetration of distance and belonging reminds Christians and churches of two important points regarding cultural identity. First, boundaries are indispensable for identity formation. With no boundaries, the world is amorphous and so is identity. Second, for interpenetration to take place boundaries have to be permeable to let the other come in.[79] Christians and churches have to embrace these two points in order to uphold their identity while including the other in a culturally diverse world. However, how do Christians and churches decide or adjust the permeability of their cultural boundaries? Walter Brueggemann once suggested, "the ongoing process of life is to come to terms with this other who will practice mutuality with us, but who at the same time stands in an incommensurate relation to us."[80] Like Brueggemann, Volf also highlights that in any society there must be concurrent commensurability and incommensurability between Christian and non-Christian value systems.[81] There is no one single appropriate way for Christians to relate to a particular culture. Based on his reading of the book of First Peter, in which the commensurability and incommensurability co-exist, Volf urges Christians and the churches to face the incommensurability by adopting a meek attitude to maintain the soft difference from the undesirable cultures.[82] On one hand, Christians should recognize themselves as aliens in the world when they are baptized into the body of Christ. Volf explains that "baptism will not do the distancing for you, but it will tell you that genuine Christian distance

77. Ibid.

78. Volf, "Theological Reflections," 271.

79. Volf, "Living," 14.

80. Brueggemann, *Covenanted Self*, 2.

81. Volf, "Soft Difference," 27.

82. Ibid. 24.

has ecclesial shape."[83] This ecclesial existence is different from the lifestyle of the larger society. On the other hand, there is an inalienable dimension of the Christian ecclesial identity that they have to love enemies and non-violence. Volf believes that these two positions together give Christians the attitude of maintaining the soft difference from incommensurate culture. In fact, these two positions constitute the spirituality which gives the "courage to assert self and the grace to abandon self to another,"[84] which could be understood as asserting and abandoning self by employing no exclusion and violence to each other. Volf also reflects on the theology of agency in relation to countering social exclusion. He states emphatically that a "catholic personality" is crucial for addressing the agency in countering the exclusive culture. To his belief, theologians should focus more on how to foster "*the kind of social agents capable of envisioning and creating just, truthful, and peaceful societies, and on shaping a cultural climate in which such agents will thrive*" (emphasis original) than on social programs.[85] The social agents need to be catholic personalities in order to envision and create such societies and cultural ambience.

Volf explains how the catholic personality in relation to the subtle distancing arose out of loyalty to God and the future. Christians should distance themselves from their own culture for the sake of the new creation of God, in which all peoples with their cultural goodness will gather around God in the *eschaton*.[86] Therefore, a catholic personality should not be exclusive, but remain open to other cultures in this world. Such distancing helps curb social exclusion in two ways. First, it creates space in us to receive the other. When one comes to Christ, there is a new creation (2 Cor 5:17). The Spirit breaks through the self-enclosed world that Christians inhabit and starts the process of transforming them into catholic personalities. This is a de-centering process that makes people more open and receptive to the other.[87] Volf claims that this formation of catholic personality is in fact a "personal microcosm of the eschatological new creation."[88] Since catholicity does not just have eschatological shape but also has ecclesial shape, Volf

83. Ibid., 19.
84. Brueggemann, *Covenanted Self*, 8.
85. Volf, *Exclusion and Embrace*, 21–22.
86. Ibid., 50–51.
87. Volf, "Vision of Embrace," 199.
88. Volf, "Theological Reflections," 272.

adds that it takes a "catholic community" to raise a catholic personality.[89] Therefore, no church in a particular culture should separate itself from churches in other cultures; otherwise it negates its own catholicity, because no one single culture is sufficient to itself. Likewise, no one single church can claim to be totally self-sufficient. Hence, every church is a catholic church in the sense that they mutually shape each other.[90] And churches should commit themselves to the multicultural and ecumenical Christian community in order to nurture catholic personalities.

Second, the distance made by the Spirit of the new creation *"entails a judgment against evil in every culture"* (emphasis original).[91] While the catholic personality stresses the openness and receptiveness to the other, Volf emphasizes that it should not be interpreted as indiscriminate and wholesale acceptance of the evils in every culture. Distance creates space not just for enrichment but also for critiquing cultural currents, which are deemed evil or contrary to Christianity. In other words, catholic personality and judgment lead Christians and churches to adjust and also assert their identity in a multicultural setting and avoid the sin of social exclusion.

To summarize, it is apparent that Volf is well aware of the impact of social exclusion on the church and society as a whole. He has contributed a thoughtful cultural analysis of social exclusion and a theological reflection on the causes, dynamics and consequences of this cultural current. His analysis and reflection reveal that he is concerned with how the culture of social exclusion impacts society as a whole, rather than just focus on how it may affect ecclesial life. In addressing social exclusion, Volf underscores the centrality of agency in countering the exclusive culture and bringing in a just and peaceful society. In this sense, it is fair to say that Volf is more countercultural than either de Lubac or Zizioulas—for Volf has a clearer understanding of the countercultural function of theology, and he is more explicit in his intention to address the cultural issues through his theology, though he might not interpret the Eucharist in this way. Further exploration is needed to see how he interprets the Eucharist in shaping both the catholic personality and the catholic community to counter social exclusion.

89. Volf, *Exclusion and Embrace*, 51.
90. Volf, "Vision of Embrace," 199.
91. Volf, *Exclusion and Embrace*, 52.

VOLF'S ADDRESS TO SOCIAL EXCLUSION

To counter the culture of social exclusion, Volf constructs the theology of embrace. This construction is based on the divine embrace of God toward alienated humanity as shown on the cross.[92] He interprets the Eucharist as the re-enactment of this divine embrace carried in the memory of the Passion to form catholic personality. Volf states that by commemorating this memory in the Eucharist, Christians are able to re-narrate the divine embrace and are formed to become catholic agents to live their lives rightly—a life of embrace to counter social exclusion in anticipation of the eschatological communion or reconciliation.[93]

Embrace: Space for others as shown in the Trinity and the Passion of the cross

Contrary to the scheme of "oppression/liberation," which primarily concentrates on the pursuit of justice, usually resulting in the irony that reconciliation is made impossible,[94] Volf proposes a new paradigm of "exclusion/embrace" to counter the exclusive culture. To curb social exclusion, Volf adopts the notion of embrace, which is a metaphor of folding the other into one's bosom, signifying reconciliation. He uses embrace to refer to creating space for the other and as a way of re-thinking personal and communal identity under the condition of enmity.[95] In order for embrace to happen there has to be "fluidity of identities" that allows negotiation of difference.[96] He also explains that the more exclusive the culture is the more rigid and impermeable one's boundary or space is to the other. Social exclusion results where negotiation and adjustment of identities *vis-à-vis* the other is made difficult, if not totally impossible. To counter social exclusion, Volf further interprets the Eucharist as the sacrament of God's embrace.[97] Before turning to Volf's connection of embrace and the Eucharist, the structure of the embrace in Volf's theology needs to be examined.

92. Volf, *Exclusion and Embrace*, 128–29.

93. Volf, "Memory, Eschatology, Eucharist," 32, 34.

94. Volf, "Theological Reflections," 268–69.

95. Volf, *Exclusion and Embrace*, 140.

96. Ibid., 145.

97. Ibid., 129.

Volf delineates how embrace metaphorically depicts creation of space for the other. In Volf's interpretation, when a person opens the arms showing the willingness to embrace, space is created for the other to enter in. In an embrace, arms are opened to the other as a sign of invitation to enter in without demolishing the other's particularity or enmeshing both parties' identities. The actual embrace is realized when both parties want to give a mutual embrace. In a mutual embrace, both parties are enriched by each other yet remain true to themselves.[98] In other words, the inclusion of the other in oneself denotes the creating of space to counter social exclusion, which is basically rejection of the other from one's symbolic cultural world and physical territory.

Volf further connects his notion of embrace to the divine embrace among the three persons in the Trinity.[99] The mutual self-donation of the divine persons forms the basis of *perichoresis*.[100] He interprets *perichoresis* of the three divine persons in the Trinity as the divine embrace or opening space of one person to the other without destroying any person's identity. Consistent with his proposal of the Trinity as the "social vision" for human beings to follow,[101] Volf proposes that this divine embrace predicates human community as an analogous imitation. Certainly, Volf does not suggest a full correspondence between embrace at the divine level and the human level, because there is no complete interiority in human beings. However, there is the interiority of personal characteristics corresponding to the divine interiority. When each person gives herself or himself to others in an encounter, "mutual interiorization of personal characteristics" occurs.[102] *Perichoresis* or the divine embrace in the Trinity and its correspondence at the human level support the important idea that identity is not self-contained. Identity is shaped by making and giving space for the other. The divine embrace implies that human identity can be shaped or negotiated by opening space for the other, which is crucial to countering social exclusion. While the interpenetration of the divine persons accounts for the catholicity of the triune God, human beings who are re-created by the Holy Spirit, begin their journey to become a catholic personality, who will analogously mirror the catholic triune God. This is the reason that Volf

98. Volf, "Vision of Embrace," 203.

99. Ibid.

100. Volf, "Trinity is Our Social Program," 412.

101. Ibid., 406.

102. Volf, *After Our Likeness*, 211.

relies not on social programs, but on the formation of social agents, who are shaped to be catholic personalities to engage in social transformation by letting others come into her or his space.

Volf further relates the embrace of the Trinity to the Passion. When the divine embrace of the persons of the Trinity turns to face the world, it is the outpouring of circular divine self-donation through the Passion of Christ on the cross to embrace alienated humanity to God's bosom. The downward movement from the circular love in the Trinity to the cross is an indiscriminate will to embrace humanity, which is in enmity with God. Furthermore, the Passion is God's embrace of solidarity with victims as well as substitution for aggressors.[103] Thus the Passion manifests God's most complete and unreserved opening of space to all humanity.

Volf regards the memory of the Passion as a powerful way to shape the identities of God's people.[104] This memory is crucial for forming agents who can facilitate the embrace against exclusion. He adopts Johannes Baptist Metz's notion of "dangerous memories" to explain his point.[105] This view maintains that from the perspective at the foot of the cross the memory of the Passion is definitely subversive, because it is a memory of suffering that demands Christians to live accordingly in their everyday lives. The memory of the Passion reminds Christians to live a life of embrace because of what the memory promises. First, unconditional grace is extended to wrongdoers. Christians are expected to imitate Christ by willingly embracing wrongdoers who reject the victims, because wrongdoers are also remembered and forgiven by God.[106] Second, while Christ died as a substitution for sinners,[107] he promises to protect the identities of victims and not allow them to be shattered by wrongdoings. Victims are also given power by the Holy Spirit to imitate God by embracing wrongdoers and struggling against injustice.[108] Third, the memory of the Passion anticipates the formation of a *"reconciled community out of deadly enemies"* (emphasis original) in the *eschaton* that both the wronged and the wrongdoers will meet and greet each other in the grand embrace in the *eschaton*.[109] Thus through the

103. Volf, "Memory, Eschatology, Eucharist," 31.

104. Volf, *End of Memory*, 111–12.

105. Metz, *Faith in History and Society*, 109.

106. Volf, "Memory, Eschatology, Eucharist," 31.

107. Volf, *Free of Charge*, 144.

108. Volf, "Memory, Eschatology, Eucharist," 31.

109. Volf, *End of Memory*, 119.

memory of the Passion, victims and aggressors are helped to embrace and reconcile with each other.

The Eucharist: The Sacrament of Embrace and Re-enactment of the Memory of the Passion

Volf connects the memory of the Passion to the Eucharist, which is the sacrament of God's embrace and the re-enactment of this memory. The re-enactment of this memory in the Eucharist shapes the identities of social agents to embrace the other amidst a culture of exclusion that has been stripped of grace. In "Theology for a Way of Life," he states unequivocally that sacraments ritually enact normative pattern for practices.[110] In other words, sacraments are understood as the embodiment of rules and resources, which are to be appropriated by Christians in their daily lives.[111]

Influenced by his Free Church heritage, Volf focuses on the two *dominic* sacraments, namely, baptism and the Eucharist. He explains how these two sacraments prescribe the way of life stipulated by core Christian beliefs in relation to the particular cultural identity of Christians. The baptismal liturgy is incorporation into the body of Christ, an ushering into the Christian community. Volf also highlights that the baptism *per se* does not do the distancing for Christians, but it emphasizes that there is authentic Christian distance from the prevailing culture of the larger society.[112]

While baptism is a one-off welcome to a new member into the Christian community, which gives the distancing an ecclesial shape,[113] the Eucharist is a repetitive reminder of such ecclesial distancing from the exclusive culture. Volf shares his personal experience and reflection of how his parents extended the unconditional divine welcome from the Table of the Lord to the dining table in their house, by giving unusual hospitality to a man who was usually not welcome in the social circle.[114] Volf emphasizes that through the sacraments Christian normative beliefs are inscribed in order to shape practices in daily life. In the Eucharist particularly the Christian norm of welcome and embrace to strangers, or those who are excluded, is inscribed.

---

110. Volf, "Way of Life," 127.

111. See Jones, "Loosing and Binding," 37.

112. Volf, "Soft Difference," 19.

113. Ibid.

114. Volf, "Way of life," 127–28.

Volf further connects the divine embrace embedded in the memory of the Passion to the Eucharist, which is a re-enactment of this memory. He explains that the cross is etched with the memory of the Passion, which is commemorated in the Eucharist. Put differently, what happened on the cross happens in the Eucharist—the divine self-donation and embrace, which are the outpouring of the perichoretic love of the Trinity through the sacrifice of Christ. Volf regards self-donation and embrace as central to the cross. And the Eucharist best re-presents this overarching significance and prescribes the believers' way of life according to the narrative of the divine action on the cross.[115] The Eucharist is crucial for Christians to live rightly by rightly remembering the Passion. Volf also points out that the reiterated celebration of the Eucharist actually re-enacts the self-giving of Christ, who sacrificed his body for people so that they can be crafted into his image. In fact, the re-enactment of the self-sacrifice of Christ at the Table is an indiscriminate invitation for all to partake in him. As such, the Eucharist is God's invitation to all to be embraced.

However, Volf cautions that it would be a grave misunderstanding to think of the Eucharist as only a sacrament of God's embrace, and that those who partake in it are purely recipients on whom no claim can be laid. As the title of Todd B. Murken's book, *Take and Eat, and Take the Consequence*, suggests, receiving the Eucharist is an act that begs to make a difference.[116] This making of differences relies on the changes in the participants. What is done to the participants in the Eucharist must also be done by them. Volf contests that participants are recipients only if they are willing to be formed into agents of the Eucharist. Accordingly, the participants in the Eucharist must impart the embrace of God to others by creating space.[117]

To facilitate creating space for others, it is instructive to recall that when Jesus invited persons to his meal who were excluded by the mainstream, social and cultural boundaries were subverted and "*redrawn inclusively*" (emphasis original) by Jesus.[118] This inclusivity expresses the internalized relations in the Body of Christ. Since the sin of exclusion is social (the injury done to the identities of human beings is a social process), therefore the healing of injury must be social.[119] The inclusive dining

---

115. Volf, "Forgiveness, Reconciliation, and Justice," 876.

116. Murken, *Take and Eat*.

117. Volf, *Exclusion and Embrace*, 129.

118. Shriver, *Ethic for Enemies*, 40.

119. Volf, "Final Reconciliation," 94.

etiquette of Jesus imbues the holy meal with socio-cultural healing and reconciliation. Moreover, this transcending of socio-cultural boundaries goes beyond today's church. In Volf's interpretation, the Eucharist, which commemorates the memory of the Passion, elicits the vision to re-narrate life in great anticipation of the new creation of humanity. In the performance of the Eucharist, there is hope of the ultimate embrace, or reconciliation, in the Kingdom of God.[120] In other words, the memory of the Passion is anticipatory of the final reconciliation of wrongdoers and victims in God's Kingdom.[121] Likewise, the Eucharist is also anticipatory; it anticipates the catholicity that culminates in the eschatological banquet.[122] Christians are on the journey toward this banquet in *finale* by analogously imitating the embrace of the Host in their ongoing life. In the Eucharist, participants envision this ultimate banquet in the Spirit, and they are on the way to become the true catholic personalities who will dine together one day. At that Table, there is no more exclusion, only embrace.

Having said that the Eucharist is the commemoration of the memory of the Passion, which is the divine embrace that counters exclusion, Volf takes note of two challenges involved, namely, forgiveness and memories of hurts inflicted by wrongdoers. With respect to forgiveness, he gives a strong reminder that the actualization of embrace is a challenge, because it will not happen until justice is done and forgiveness is granted and accepted. "Forgiveness is the boundary between exclusion and embrace," says Volf.[123] It is true that forgiveness helps overcome this boundary and heals the wounds caused by social exclusion. Forgiveness also helps facilitate aggressors and victims to move across the space between them for mutual embrace. However, Volf stresses that the pursuit of justice cannot be abandoned for the sake of cheap forgiveness. He also points out that "first justice, then forgiveness" is not workable to the same degree as the scheme of "first justice, then reconciliation."[124] After all, Volf's notion of forgiveness is a gift of victims to wrongdoers. He argues that forgiveness is grace and justice should be subordinate to grace.[125] If strict forgiveness could be done at all, and the damages caused by the wrongdoers could be fully redressed, the

---

120. Volf, "Memory, Eschatology, Eucharist," 32.

121. Volf, *End of Memory*, 119.

122. Volf, *Exclusion and Embrace*, 130.

123. Ibid., 125.

124. Volf, "Forgiveness, Reconciliation, and Justice," 871.

125. Volf, "Social Meaning of Reconciliation," 165, 167.

wronged one would not need to extend this gift—no gift would be needed. Nor would the wrongdoer need forgiveness in this case, for he or she had already paid all dues. Yet, Volf is not suggesting that forgiveness should be granted regardless of justice just for the sake of embrace. Actually he suggests putting the concern of justice under the primacy of the will to embrace or to have reconciliation. At the same time, Volf stresses forgiveness is possible only if there is "tacit affirmation of justice."[126] The delicate tension between affirmation of justice and the granting of forgiveness makes the actual embrace a challenge.

Another challenge to the actual embrace is the memories of wrongdoings. Volf does not take lightly the impact of such memory on the difficulty of embrace. He is well aware that the memories of wrongdoings have afflicted the victims, inhibited forgiveness, and also endangered their identities, since memories are significant in shaping identity. Memories can be complicated and emotionally charged, especially memories of wrongdoings. Any attempt to generalize how people remember or even forget may risk the accusation of being too simplistic and insensitive. Given the constraints of this chapter, it is impossible to give a full-fledged analysis of Volf's theology of memory. It suffices to highlight how Volf tackles the inextricable relationship between forgiveness of aggressors and the memories of sufferings. He suggests reframing the memories of the wrongdoings under the overarching framework of the memory of the Passion.[127] Such reframing is not the eradication of the memories of wrongdoings. Rather it is the conferring of meanings, which constitute implications to the beholders of profane memories. This is in order to protect their well-being, while they await the eschatological Kingdom of perfect embrace and love to come.

In a nutshell, Volf advocates that memories of wrongdoings can be reframed under the lens of the Passion memory, which anticipates the final judgment and final reconciliation to come. Through remembering rightly under the lens of the memory of the Passion, Volf argues that the wronged victims can draw resources from this memory to live their lives in great anticipation of the final judgment and reconciliation.[128] This reframing of hurting memories is not the removal of memories of wrongdoings. Volf maintains that to remember rightly means to hold on to the memory of wrongdoings until its purpose of serving as a guardian against future hurts

126. Volf, "Forgiveness, Reconciliation, and Justice," 874.

127. Volf, *End of Memory*, 124–25.

128. Volf, "God's Forgiveness and Ours," 220.

and a servant of justice is no longer needed. Volf is emphatic that this purpose will be accomplished only:

> *After* (emphasis original) Christ has completed the work of salvation and the eschatological transition has taken place, *after* (emphasis original) the wrongdoers and the wronged have entered that world which cannot be undone—*after* (emphasis original) the Last Judgment, *after* (emphasis original) wrong committed and suffered has come to public light in God's judgment of grace, *after* (emphasis original) the perpetrators have been accused and the victims vindicated, *after* (emphasis original) they have embraced each other and recognized each other as belonging to the same community of perfect love, *after* (emphasis original) all these occurrences—the memories of wrongs suffered will be released. They will no longer come to mind to diminish the joy that each person will know in the presence of others and all will know in the presence of God.[129]

Volf contests that in the future world of perfect love, there is no point to reject such "non-remembrance"[130] of wrongdoings—the "'not-coming-to-mind' of wrongs suffered after justice has been served and after entrance into a secure world of perfect love."[131] Assuming Volf is understood correctly here, however, one has to ask the question: who will receive God's judgment of grace to enter into such a secure world of perfect love? If not all will be recipients of the judgment of grace, then some wrongdoers will not be released from guilt and be transformed, and thus will not participate in the mutual embrace in the *eschaton*. If plenary mutual embrace between the aggressors and the victims is not possible in the *eschaton*, what will happen to the profane memories the perpetrator causes the victim? Will there be non-remembering of those memories, as Volf has suggested? Only if Volf believes in universal salvation, will there be plenary mutual embrace leading to non-remembrance of wrongdoings. However, he is silent on this point. Regrettably, Volf only makes a passing remark, without disclosing and discussing his viewpoint or arguments concerning universal salvation and its impact on embrace and reconciliation.[132] He leaves a big loophole,

---

129. Volf, *End of Memory*, 182–83.

130. Ibid., 145. Volf deliberately uses the "not-coming-to-mind" to smooth out the negative connotation of "forgetting."

131. Ibid., 203.

132. Ibid., 180.

or even an Achilles' heel, in his theological explanation of the relationship between forgiveness, memories, and final reconciliation.

In the final analysis, Volf counters the culture of social exclusion by interpreting the Eucharist as the sacrament of God's embrace and the re-enactment of the Passion memory. It is the manifestation of the divine embrace to heal social exclusion. Volf is also aware of the complexities of forgiveness as well as memories of wrongdoings, which may render a full embrace a challenge in the present world. He recommends that the primacy of the will to embrace and by rightly remembering wrongs through the lens of the Passion can provide sustaining power to the victims to seek healing and peace while they await the final judgment and reconciliation.

THE COUNTERCULTURAL FUNCTION OF THE EUCHARIST ACCORDING TO VOLF'S INTERPRETATION

At the risk of being repetitious, it is imperative to point out that Volf employs the Eucharist as the formation of catholic personality, which he thinks to have critical importance in countering the exclusive culture. He is concerned with nurturing catholic agents who can envisage and construct peaceful and reconciling societies on shaping cultural ambience in which such agents will thrive.[133] Volf regards the Eucharist as creating cultural impact against the exclusive culture through the catholic personality. However, when Volf's interpretation of the Eucharist is put into the broader context of his theological system there is ambiguity in ascertaining the significance of the Eucharist *vis-à-vis* the culture. This is because the Eucharist does not occupy a central position in his theological system. While Volf is laborious in doing cultural analysis of social exclusion in order to engender a theological account of the exclusive culture, he responds to this issue of the Eucharist without substantially delineating his theology concerning this liturgy. The disparity between his well elaborated analysis of social exclusion and his comparatively modest theological account of the Eucharist *per se* must be considered in light of a comparison between Catholic and Orthodox traditions. Only then may this disparity be explained by the relative lack of emphasis on sacraments and also the rather one-sided emphasis on the individualistic interpretation of the Eucharist in the Protestant tradition. Even though Volf acknowledges that the core beliefs directing Christian practices are inscribed in the sacraments, the Eucharist is still

133. Volf, *Exclusion and Embrace*, 21.

hardly at the center of his theology. Further evaluation of Volf's elucidation of the Eucharist in countering social exclusion is necessary to assess the validity of his elucidation.

First, based on his construction of the theology of embrace to heal social exclusion, Volf connects embrace to the Eucharist, which is the sacrament of God's embrace.[134] However, the recognition of the Eucharist as the sacrament of God's embrace is actually an ecumenical effort or consensus and is not original to Volf. *Baptism, Eucharist and Ministry (BEM)* states that:

> The Eucharist embraces all aspects of life . . . . All kinds of injustice, racism, separation and lack of freedom are radically challenged when we share in the body and blood of Christ . . . . As participants in the Eucharist, therefore, we prove inconsistent if we are not actively participating in this ongoing restoration of the world's situation and the human condition.[135]

Since Volf does not formulate a full theological account of the Eucharist in his system, his use of the Eucharist as the sacrament of God's embrace and reconciliation actually gains validity on the basis of ecumenical recognition of the Eucharist as quoted above. It is just to say that the validity of Volf's countering of social exclusion by means of the Eucharist is not so much credited by a full interpretation of the Eucharist in his theology (which he has not done, actually) as by his implicit dependence on the ecumenical acknowledgement of the Eucharist as the sacrament of God's embrace. Inversely, Volf divulges that he borrowed from ecumenical input regarding the Eucharist to validate his address to social exclusion.

A second assessment of Volf's validity in redressing social exclusion is how he explains the formation of catholic personality, which, according to him, is crucial to transforming the exclusionary culture. A closer look at his explanation indicates that it is rather unclear how he actually draws from the Protestant tradition to support the formation of catholic personality. No wonder Curtis Freeman suggests that Volf should consider more about the sacraments by having conversations with other theologians who are more interested in sacramental ecclesiology.[136] After emphasizing the need of catholic agent, he swiftly claims both Catholic and Orthodox traditions for support. He briefly cites Hans Urs von Balthasar and John Zizioulas to

---

134. Ibid., 128–29.

135. World Council of Churches, *Baptism, Eucharist, and Ministry*, 14.

136. Freeman, "Gathered," 268.

support the significance of catholic personality around the Eucharist in the long tradition of the Catholic Church and the Orthodox Church respectively. Comparatively speaking, Volf draws a little bit more support from Zizioulas than from Balthasar.[137] He adopts Zizioulas's idea of the ecclesial or catholic person to develop the concept of catholic personality, which is crucial to his construction of the theology of embrace to counter social exclusion.[138] In a rather broad stroke, Volf connects the Eucharist to the catholic personality by portraying it as the anticipation of the eschatological gathering of God's people in the new creation. As such, the Holy Spirit sets God's people on the way to become truly catholic agents. He goes on to say:

> In the Eucharist, then, we celebrate the giving of the self to the other and the receiving of the other into the self that the triune God has undertaken in the passion of Christ and that we are called and empowered to live such giving and receiving out in a conflict-ridden world.[139]

Volf could have made his idea of the catholic personality more explicit by elucidating how the emergence of the catholic personality is a spiritual formation nourished by the Eucharist, especially in light of the fact that he maintains that Christians are called and empowered to live the way of life, which is actually discipleship, by participating in the Eucharist (see above quote). Yet, he has not done so sufficiently. It may be due to the fact that though Volf emphasizes the Eucharist as *esse* of the church, as a Protestant theologian he has not developed his theology of sacrament in full, like the theologians from the Catholic and the Orthodox traditions have done. The link between the sacraments and Christian living or discipleship needs to be further concretized theologically. His connection of the Eucharist to the catholic personality still needs support from other traditions to make it more adequate.

In addition to what Zizioulas teaches about catholic personality, another Catholic theologian, Philip Sheldrake, has written prolifically on spirituality. His body of work is a possible resource that can help concretize Volf's idea of catholic personality. In particular, Sheldrake's interpretation of the Eucharist as the practicing of catholic place is complementary to Volf's "embrace as creating space for the other" as far as distance and

137. Volf, *Exclusion and Embrace*, 129.
138. Zizioulas, *Being as Communion*, 58.
139. Volf, *Exclusion and Embrace*, 130.

belonging with respect to culture is concerned. The ability of Christians to grasp and embody the spirit of distance and belonging in different cultures is precisely what discipleship is all about and is crucial for them to live as catholic agents. Moreover, Sheldrake's interpretation of "the Eucharist as ethical space" can buttress Volf's idea of forming catholic personality.[140]

While Volf focuses on embrace, which is creation of space for the other, Sheldrake puts the primary emphasis on place since place precedes space, and place is one of the universal cultural categories, and crucial for establishing identity and relationship.[141] To Sheldrake, place is more than location and physical features; its significance depends more on relationships and memories connected to localities and socio-cultural conditions.[142] Contrary to the notion of space, which is abstract, Sheldrake interprets place in theological terms as particular. Place, being God's creation and therefore particular, can give a sense of belonging, which simultaneously excludes the other. A particular place, whether it is physically or culturally referred to, always carries "thisness," which is specific and exclusive.[143] However, due to the absolute inclusivity of God or the absolute catholicity, which is only applicable to God,[144] he encompasses all particular places. Sheldrake argues that a theology of place is necessary to sustain the balance between God's revelation in the particular and his catholicity, which is not bound by localized boundaries.[145] This balance should be accurately understood as a dynamic co-existence of the particular and the going beyond of the particular. This dynamic notion of balance is complementary to Volf's relative static idea of distance and belonging regarding culture. In fact, the validity of Volf's account of forming catholic agents to countering social exclusion hinges on how he can interpret the Eucharist as the spiritual formation of the faithful to dynamically live the spirit of distance and belonging in the midst of different cultures.

More importantly, Sheldrake's own understanding of discipleship in relation to place is in fact a core matter of spiritual formation, on which point Volf is not explicit enough. Sheldrake regards discipleship as a simultaneous demand for a place and a "further." He elucidates his notion

140. Sheldrake, *Spaces*, 75.

141. Ibid., 4, 7.

142. Ibid., 8.

143. Ibid., 25.

144. Ibid., 29.

145. Ibid., 30.

of discipleship by quoting De Certeau; that it is a Christian experience in which "boundaries are the place of the Christian work, and their displacements are the result of this work."[146] Discipleship is best understood as the practice of catholicity that actually drives Christians to move on to embrace the elsewhere or the other. The overcoming of boundaries includes not just time and place but also natural or cultural differences between people. By using discipleship to explain the practice of catholicity, Sheldrake, as suggested by Volf, increases the formation of catholic agents who are imbued with a greater sense of intention and accountability in their identity as Disciples of Christ in two ways. First, the practicing of catholicity of place is discipleship as "doing Christ,"[147] which is a continuous formation. Sheldrake explicates that discipleship is precisely a practice of catholic place—having placedness given by God's commitment through Jesus while moving "further" or to "elsewhere."[148] Such placedness and moving on was embodied by the life of the incarnated Son and his embrace toward those who were on the margin of society. Second, Sheldrake's exposition of "ethical sacramentality,"[149] which is internal to the Eucharist, can further strengthen the ethical dimension of Volf's idea of formation of catholic personality. Sheldrake argues from the point of view of sacramental theology, in that "a truly sacramental view is necessary to an ethical view and vice versa."[150] If he is understood correctly, Christian worship and especially the Eucharist, which is the sacrament *par excellence,* must entail a way of life appropriated by worship and the Eucharist.[151] From the Eucharist as the catholic place comes precisely the sacramental-ethic of embracing the other as a way of life. Sheldrake elaborates this point more explicitly than Volf, that such ethical sacramentality leading to embrace is not so much an ethical "responsibility for" the other as a "responsibility with" the other. This responsibility with the other nurtures mutual embrace since everyone simultaneously sins and is sinned against. Under the framework of responsibility with the other, mutual love is called and empowered by the practice of catholic place in the Eucharist. This framework makes the mutual embrace, which Volf has emphatically suggested, more possible

146. Ibid., 31.
147. Ibid., 69.
148. Ibid., 64.
149. Ibid., 74–75.
150. Ibid., 74.
151. See Saliers, "Liturgy and Ethics," 5.

because it underscores the mutual accountability. In this way, Sheldrake's emphasis on the practice of catholic place in the Eucharist as discipleship, that is, the spiritual formation of catholicity provides a more active ethical tenor to Volf's idea of formation of catholic personality. As such, the validity of Volf's address to social exclusion by means of the Eucharist can be enhanced by borrowing from the ethical sacramentality in the Catholic tradition of sacramental theology.

Finally, the validity of the enactment of the Passion memory in the Eucharist to counter social exclusion is not without limits. Although Volf anticipates that the memory of the Passion will be re-enacted and internalized by participants in the Eucharist, he hardly supports this through liturgical texts or protocols from the Protestant tradition. He is rather quiescent on how the participants remember the Passion. Memory is complicated and can be tricky. It is not a single, isolated function of the brain; it is multifaceted.[152] For example, Andrea Bieler and Luise Schottroff argue that remembering or *anamnesis* is a complex process in which body memory, cultural memory, and place memory are brought to the Table of the Lord where they all intermingle.[153] The meaning of the Passion memory generated from the performance of the Eucharist may also depend on personal life stories viewed against the background of the larger social and political context in which one finds oneself.[154] For example, one interesting qualification to Volf's proposal of the enactment of the memory of the Passion in the Eucharist is the Irish Catholic Eucharist described and explained by Christian Scharen.[155] Scharen cites the case study by the ethnographer Siobhán Garrigan. In Garrigan's study, the members of an Irish Catholic Church only took the bread. The non-reception of the cup was actually a body memory of this congregation. This body memory of the non-reception of the cup in this particular Irish Catholic congregation has nothing to do with the Vatican II re-introduction of observing both kinds. Rather, it is in response and resistance to the British accusation of being drunkards—a label the British oppressors used to smear their reputation. What this Irish Catholic Eucharist re-enacted was not really the memory of the Passion but the memory of ancient social exclusion by the British aggressors. This case study serves as an instructive reminder that the enactment of the memory

---

152. Bieler and Schottroff, *The Eucharist*, 175.

153. Ibid., 173.

154. Ibid.

155. See Scharen, "Ecclesiology 'From the Body,'" 59–61.

of the Passion in the Eucharist may need to be scrutinized against the body memory and cultural memory of the participants. Put differently, the body memory and the cultural memory call for subtle consideration when one is trying to exact what the Eucharist re-enacts and thus what meaning it actually engenders. Otherwise, an over-simplification of what the Eucharist commemorates may lead to a risk of over-generalization of the enactment of the Passion memory at the Lord's Table. This possible risk is an inadequacy in Volf's move to counter social exclusion through the memory of the Passion re-enacted in the Eucharist. Volf's rather opaque description of how the performance of the Eucharist can be a commemoration may be due to the lack of liturgical theology and rubric in the Protestant tradition (especially the Free Church) in comparison to the Catholic and the Orthodox traditions.

In addition to the questions of validity concerning how Volf uses the Eucharist to address social exclusion, there is a related concern about the actual practice. Does Volf agree to the practice of excluding those who have not been baptized from receiving the Eucharist? Volf is peculiarly silent on this issue. It is difficult to comprehend why he is completely quiet about this kind of exclusion after being so sensitive to the exclusionary culture. On the contrary, Moltmann, whose doctrine of perichoretic Trinity has been adopted by Volf to formulate the theology of embrace, advocates open invitation to the Eucharist.[156]

SUMMARY

This examination of Volf's theological system has shown that his doctrines of the Trinity and ecclesiology are not characteristically eucharistic. Still, he posits the Eucharist as *esse* of the church and interprets it as the prescription of embracing the other as the Christian way of life, opposing the exclusive culture. Volf's theology of embrace adds to the church understanding of the sin of social exclusion against humanity. His reliance on catholic personality but not social programs to countering social exclusion is an instructive reminder to the church that it takes the right kind of personality to bear witness to the world, not just social initiatives. His emphasis on forming catholic agents also alerts the Christian communities to remember that in Christianity, formation of personality is always part and parcel of spiritual formation even though Volf does not use this term explicitly enough. Still,

---

156. Moltmann, *Church in Power*, 246.

in Volf's connection of the Eucharist to the formation of catholic agents, there is potential to further concretize this formation. Thus, this research suggests Sheldrake's interpretation of the Eucharist as the practice of catholicity and nurturing of disciples, which is a core matter of spiritual formation, to explicate what Volf has been less vocal about in this regard. Finally, the validity and effectiveness of Volf's interpretation of the Eucharist might have been even more substantiated if he could more specifically mention the ritual-liturgical dimension of the Eucharist according to his own Protestant tradition. Especially, he has to explain more concretely how the memory of the Passion is re-enacted in the Eucharist in the Free Church tradition in order to explicate the kind of impact he expects participants to have on mainstream culture.

6

A Comparative Evaluation

THIS CHAPTER CONSTRUCTS A comparative evaluation of de Lubac, Zizioulas, and Volf concerning their ways and efforts in countering the cultural currents by their interpretations of the Eucharist. This comparative evaluation includes the following four aspects: their awareness of cultural currents; their diagnoses of cultural currents; the correlation of their interpretations of the Eucharist to cultural currents; and the effectiveness of countering cultural currents by their interpretations.

AWARENESS OF CULTURAL CURRENTS

A theologian's awareness of cultural currents does not come from nowhere. It is shaped by a number of factors; for example, the socio-cultural context in which the theologian is situated, his or her personal life experience, theological career and church tradition, to name just a few. All these factors have an integral impact on the horizon from which theologians look at the cultural milieu and define their alertness to any cultural problems. De Lubac, Zizioulas, and Volf's awareness of cultural currents exemplifies this integral influence. It is helpful to look into details about their alertness to the cultural currents of their times and also the factors shaping their awareness.

In the case of Zizioulas, his responsiveness to the exploitive culture on nature, which has caused the global ecological crisis, as well as the ecumenical dialogue, has been a long-term endeavor that can be traced back to the early stage of his theological career. A brief recapitulation of Zizioulas's theological career will prove this point. He has been involved in ecumenical circles since he was a graduate student at the universities of Thessalonika and Athens from 1950–1954. Later he became the founding member of the International Joint Commission for Theological Dialogue with the Catholic Church, and he was also the co-chairman of the international Anglican-Orthodox dialogue in 1979. His ample and active interaction with different cultures in the ecumenical family has equipped him with a global perspective, enabling him to be progressive in respect of the ecological crisis. He regards this crisis as global and cultural, overshadowing the whole world.[1] Zizioulas's theological engagement with the ecological crisis is not just an academic *ethos*. His engagement is shaped by the long tradition of the Orthodox Church in envisioning the cosmos as liturgy, meaning a "cosmic liturgy that offers the whole of creation before the throne of God."[2] Zizioulas's theological vision concerning the ecological crisis has been a long term endeavor exemplified by his three remarkable academic publications, namely, "The Eucharistic Vision of the World and Contemporary Humanity" (1966), "Preserving God's Creation: Three Lectures on Theology and Ecology," (1989) and *The Eucharistic Communion and the World* (2011). These three works span a period of more than three decades. Deeply rooted in the Orthodox heritage, Zizioulas strongly suggests the complete demarcation between supernatural-natural in western theology, which has led to the desacralization of creation and leads to the exploitive culture impacting creation. It is imperative to point out that Zizioulas's alertness to the individualistic culture is closely connected to his foresight concerning the environmental pandemic. He understands the triune God as a communion of three persons who draw humanity and all creation into the Trinity. The individualistic cultural current of humanity draws human beings away from this communion with God and creation. An exploitive attitude toward nature results an ecological crisis.

Given the fact that Zizioulas's alertness to the ecological crisis is aroused by his subscription to the patristic teachings concerning the non-separation of the supernatural-natural, it would be reasonable for him to pose a question to de Lubac. De Lubac had been a leading figure in the New Theology movement and had fought a long hard battle arguing for a connection between nature and supernatural. Why then, did he not

1. Zizioulas, *Eucharistic Communion and World*, 143.
2. Ibid., 123.

unequivocally include the nonhuman nature part of creation in his publications? If he insisted that nature and the supernatural are inseparable, and if he fought for so long against the Neo-Thomist extrinsicist view of the supernatural/natural held by his fellow theologians, then why did he show no ecological concerns?

At the risk of being repetitious, it is necessary to point out that a theologian's awareness of a cultural current is affected by many different factors. It is just to defend de Lubac on this point. In his particular early 1900s context he was far more alarmed by the mounting pressures of totalitarianism, Nazism, and Fascism. This political trio brooded over Europe in an atmosphere of war. In this cultural milieu, the rather complacent and remote attitude of the Catholic Church contributed to the rise of individualistic piety. This peculiar context and his personal experience of wars and those totalitarian regimes caused de Lubac to be more aware of totalitarianism and hierarchical culture, while he was quiet about the less imminent ecological issue. This particular context can also explain why the other theologians of de Lubac's time were not alert to ecological problems.

In a similar vein, Volf's awareness of social exclusion is significantly shaped by his personal experience of exclusion due to his Protestant background, because he was brought up in predominantly Catholic or Orthodox areas. Moreover, as a Croatian, he has more heartfelt feelings toward the genocides in Europe. This particular context in Europe, together with his personal experiences, primed Volf to cautiously address the damages brought about by the cultural current of social exclusion. Furthermore, his theological vision of an ecclesiology for the Free Church, based on a more egalitarian and reciprocal trinitarian model, sharpens his sensitivity to combat social exclusion by constructing a social model of the Trinity.

DIAGNOSIS OF CULTURAL CURRENTS

Both de Lubac and Zizioulas are concerned with individualistic culture. In diagnosing this cultural current, Zizioulas shows a more refined analysis than de Lubac. While de Lubac just acknowledges the individualistic cultural current in both society and the church, he makes neither a theological nor social detailed analysis. He simply takes it as a universal phenomenon and says that it is impossible to give one single factor or formula for it.[3] Reasonably speaking, no one would expect him to give an analysis

3. De Lubac, *Catholicism,* 168.

of this cultural current based on one single factor; individualistic cultural current can be multifaceted. Perhaps de Lubac presumes that other people acknowledge this cultural current in the same way he does. Instead of attempting a diagnosis using different analytical tools or theories, de Lubac is more apt to take a stance arguing that the church cannot be immune to this cultural current outside its walls. He suggests two reasons for the infiltration of the individualistic current into the church. First, the church overstated her ability to offer effective resistance to the individualistic current. Second, the church over emphasized the eucharistic realism, which resulted in downplaying the ecclesial realism of the Eucharist. This underemphasis of ecclesial realism causes the loss of the sense of unity. However, de Lubac shows less analytical clarity of individualism than Zizioulas does. Compared to Zizioulas's diagnosis of the individualistic cultural trend, de Lubac gives an impression of brevity.

Though Zizioulas does not go into detailed differentiation of the individualistic cultural current and its causes (for example, compare what Robert Bellah has done),[4] he attempts to diagnose this cultural current from the perspective of patristic tradition. He puts human beings under the lens of otherness, which is based on the communion of otherness among the three divine persons. According to Zizioulas, the individualistic culture results from the pursuit of "freedom from the other," while communion is "freedom for the other."[5] It is obvious that Zizioulas adopts the ontological language of uniqueness and particularity of human beings to explain that individualism is to seek freedom from the uniqueness and particularity of others.

In Zizioulas's diagnosis of the individualistic cultural current, the concern for individuality provides further comparison and conversation with de Lubac. Zizioulas considers individualism, or the individualistic cultural current, against collectivism. He explains: "Contemporary humans live every day under the weight of the opposition between the individual and the collective."[6] It is possible that violent reaction against collectivism can lead to individualism and *vice versa*. The ways in which Zizioulas puts individualism and collectivism into mutual tension are worthy of further exploration. Note that collectivism can be hegemony against individuality. The hegemonic force of collectivism suppresses or controls the individual-

---

4. Bellah, "Return of Religion, 41–42.
5. Zizioulas, *Communion and Otherness*, 9.
6. Zizioulas, *Eucharistic Communion and World*, 128.

ity of human beings in the name of a collective goal. To resist collectivism, the individualistic cultural current that upholds individuality emerges. From Zizioulas's perspective, individuality is associated with separation and death. It is exclusive to a catholic mode of existence and causes division, which leads to individualism. In order to counter the individualistic culture, individuality has to be transformed into the catholic mode of existence by ecclesial hypostasization.[7] Yet in de Lubac's analysis of the individualistic cultural trend, he does not touch on individuality. Thus, little is known about how he may handle division or difference, which is crucial to both individuality and the individualistic cultural current.

Another noteworthy point concerning both de Lubac and Zizioiulas's diagnosis of the individualistic cultural current is that both are more keenly interested in discussing the growing impact of the individualistic culture on the church than how it prevails in the larger society. De Lubac concentrates on the individualistic piety reflected by believers who take the Eucharist as private devotion. Zizioulas is concerned with the individualistic piety and pride through ascetic practices that may lead to "spiritual elitism and individualism."[8] In comparison, Volf looks at social exclusion beyond the church and its impact on the larger society in more detail, and he is concerned with how the church can take part in creating a more just and peaceful world. Comparatively speaking, Volf has shown a wider consideration of the impact of social exclusion on society than that of the individualistic culture identified by either de Lubac or Zizioulas.

While de Lubac and Zizioulas examine the issue of individualistic culture more theologically and focus on its impact on the church, Volf's diagnosis of social exclusion exemplifies how a cultural current can be examined from multiple angles. This is helpful because cultural currents are usually multi-dimensional. The starting point of Volf's analysis of social exclusion is not its impact on ecclesial communities. He first engages in a cultural analysis of social exclusion in the larger society. Instead of merely discussing social exclusion in general, he surveys the multifaceted experience of exclusion in society, paying attention to its different appearances and subtleties.[9] Based on these different forms, Volf offers his cultural analysis of social exclusion: the escalating transgression of "fault-lines"[10]

7. Zizioulas, *Being as Communion*, 58.

8. Zizioulas, *Lectures*, 125.

9. Volf, *Exclusion and Embrace*, 64–68.

10. Volf, "Vision of Embrace," 196.

of rigid "symbolic cultural maps" to expel others who do not belong or are not allowed to get into those maps.[11] Instead of focusing on how these different forms of social exclusion may have impacted the churches, he proposes questions to the ecclesial communities, inviting them to critique themselves—whether they are responsible for the exclusive culture because of the rigid cultural identity badges of Christianity they put on themselves, or because of their failure to be catholic agents to promote peace and reconciliation. Then he explains theologically that such phenomena are actually expressions of violent dis-configurations of God's creation, which is purported to be inter-dependent. After diagnosing the cultural current of exclusion from various angles, such as social phenomenon, cultural, ecclesiastical, and theological, Volf further ventures to raise the need of cultural negotiation between the identity of Christians and the mainstream culture through the notion of "soft difference,"[12] or the dialectical "distance and belonging."[13] This soft distance is actually an ongoing process of cultural negotiation between Christian's allegiance exclusive to the Kingdom of God and the catholicity of Christ, who encompasses all cultures. Since cultural negotiation is an ongoing process, there are at least two implications. First, theologians are challenged to review their tendency to focus on generalities and abstract claims. In order to contribute to the cultural negotiations of Christians in their own contexts and specificities, theologians have to learn to think and talk in the same terms and to correct opinions to which general Christians or even "popular theologies" may subscribe.[14] Second, churches need to ask how they can guide the faithful to engage in discerning the distance and belonging in their day-to-day lives. They are the subjects actually involved in endorsing or countering the cultural current prevailing in their society. Volf astutely notes that such forming and shaping takes ecclesial form, and he advocates the formation of catholic personality to counter social exclusion. In diagnosing social exclusion, Volf focuses on the importance of agency rather than social programs. In the same vein, Zizioulas does not believe that legal rules and moral instructions can help counter ecological crisis and individualism; he believes in the internalized *ethos*. De Lubac, however, is quiescent on the agency issue in overcoming the individualistic cultural current.

11. Volf, *Exclusion and Embrace*, 78.

12. Volf, "Soft Difference," 15.

13. Volf, "Vision of Embrace," 197.

14. Tanner, *Theories of Culture*, 84–85.

The above discussion shows that practically speaking, de Lubac does not really furnish a cultural analysis from a broader perspective; he is more concerned with the impact of individualism on ecclesial life. De Lubac's absence of analytical clarity in his diagnosis may be due to the fact that during his lifetime, cultural or social analysis was not quite yet the theological tool for approaching a cultural current as it is today. However, it is just to say that de Lubac alerted his contemporary world to the rise of the individualistic culture; he was prophetic in this sense. Though Zizioulas also starts with looking at how the individualistic culture affects the church, his analysis of the ecological crisis caused by the exploitative culture on environment reflects his global perspective. He offers theological analysis, which is rooted in the patristic doctrine of creation and its relation to the triune God. As for Volf, he shows how intricate a cultural current can be. He investigates social exclusion from different angles as well as the impact on society and the church. As such, Volf shows a stronger sense of being countercultural than either Zizioulas or de Lubac regarding the diagnosis of cultural currents.

CORRELATION OF THE INTERPRETATIONS OF THE EUCHARIST TO CULTURAL CURRENTS

This section makes a comparative evaluation of the validity of these three theologians' correlation between the Eucharist and cultural currents. The purpose is to highlight the ways in which they interpret the countercultural function of the Eucharist and how they may challenge or endorse each other's interpretations. Although these three theologians come from different traditions and identify different cultural currents in different contexts, they all use the doctrine of the Trinity in their interpretation of the Eucharist and ecclesiology. De Lubac explains the Eucharist as the sacrament which unities the faithful in Christ, who incorporates them into the Trinity. Zizioulas argues that the trinitarian doctrine is decisive to ecclesiology, which is inseparable from the Eucharist. Volf focuses on the outpouring of the perichoretic love of the Trinity on the cross re-enacted in the Eucharist. Therefore, it seems advisable to adopt the trinitarian framework as a common plane for this comparison. There is another reason for adopting this approach. As suggested by R. Gabriel Pivarnik in his multi-dimensional interpretation of the doctrine of the Trinity, the "trinitarain narrative" is the "overarching narrative" in interpreting and understanding the Eucharist.[15] In particular, the trinitarian participation in the Eucharist is an important foundation for its countercultural function. The faithful must participate in the Eucharist, which is imbued with the trinitarian participation, in order to be formed with dispositions in countering cultural trends in society that run contrary to Christian identity and values. It is important to remember that the Eucharist is not a communitarian liturgy made effectual merely by the participation of a group of Christians; it has a divine foundation—the trinitarian God. It is the trinitarian participation in the Eucharist that effectuates it in order to allow the faithful to participate in the life of the Divine. Both the trinitarian participation and the participation of the faithful in the Divine life within the Eucharist produce transformation; this may be called unity,[16] or eucharistic *ethos*[17] or catholic personality.[18] Such transformation has a social impact that flows from the religious realm into people's ordinary lives, including political, social, and economic life aspects.[19] Based on these reasons, the "trinitarian narrative," as the foundation of liturgical participation of the triune God, is adopted here as the common plane of comparative evaluation. The relationship between the trinitarian narrative and the Eucharist is employed as the basis of discussion concerning how the three theologians address the different interpretations of the Eucharist in relation to cultural currents.[20] The comparative evaluation will center on the validity of how they have related the trinitarian participation in the Eucharist to the formation of the faithful to express their faith in countering cultural currents through their participation in the Liturgy.

Since Pivarnik recognizes that the trinitarian narrative is multi-dimensional enough to hold both the multi-aspects of the Divine participation and the laity's participation in the liturgical action,[21] he proposes, for the purpose of comparison, four aspects of the Divine participation: "metaphysical (in the order of nature/being), soteriological (in the order

---

15. Pivarnik, *Trinitarian Theology*, xxi.

16. De Lubac, *Catholicism*, 54.

17. Zizioulas, *Communion and Otherness*, 88.

18. Volf, *Exclusion and Embrace*, 51.

19. Pivarnik, *Trinitarian Theology*, 9.

20. This method of comparing the three theologians is inspired by and adapted from Pivarnik's work on the trinitarian narrative and its relation to liturgical participation of the triune God.

21. Pivarnik, *Trinitarian Theology*, xxi.

of grace), ecclesiological (in the order of communion), and ritual-liturgical (in the order of activity)."[22] Pivarnik delineates the inextricable connection of these four aspects:

> Through the sacramental life (liturgical) of the gathered church (ecclesiological) one participates in the divine life of God who created us (metaphysical) and is thus transformed in grace for beatitude (soteriological).[23]

Accordingly, the comparative evaluation of the correlation between the theological interpretation of the Eucharist and cultural currents will be conducted around the trinitarian participation in the first three aspects suggested by Pivarnik, namely, the metaphysical, the soteriological, and the ecclesiological. Since the ritual-liturgical aspect is related to the actual performance and impact of the liturgy, this aspect will be discussed in the comparative evaluation of the effectiveness of the Eucharist in countering cultural currents.

Metaphysical Aspect (in the Order of Nature/Being)

Among these three theologians, Zizioulas gives the most overt and detailed account of how to connect the trinitarian communion to creation. His emphasis on the trinitarian doctrine is clearly noted in the beginning of chapter 4, which examines his theology of the Eucharist. He maintains that the doctrine of Trinity is indispensable in giving meaning to humanity, because the trinitarian doctrine constitutes personhood, which is crucial to all human concerns. He subscribes to the personal-hypostatic doctrine of the Trinity in which the Father is the *monarchia* that causes the Son and the Spirit to exist (outside the category of time) while they condition the Father. The *monarchia* is the *arche* that maintains the unity of the Trinity. The three divine persons maintain their own otherness while they are drawn to each other in perfect love. The Trinity is a perfect communion of the three divine persons without removing each other's particularity and uniqueness. As such, the Trinity is a primordial one-and-the-many or a perfect communion of otherness. Under the person-hypostatic doctrine of the Trinity, humanity is created by the triune God as persons by being hypostasized through Christ in the power of the Holy Spirit. Because of the

22. Ibid., 2.
23. Ibid., 5.

love of the Father extended to humanity through christological and pneumatological hypostasization, human beings participate in the trinitarian communion of otherness. Thus, the creation of human beings is trinitarian. In the same way, human beings participate in the Trinity through hypostasization through the unique hypostasis of the Son in the Holy Spirit. Zizioulas argues that since the Eucharist is the communion of the three divine persons without compromising their otherness, the Eucharist embodies this trinitarian way of existence.[24] In other words, when the faithful participate in the Eucharist, which is the summit of the trinitarian communion, they participate in a communion of otherness. The Eucharist, as a communion of otherness based on the Trinity, is the most important theological foundation that Zizioulas uses in interpreting the Liturgy to counter the individualistic culture and the exploitive cultural trend toward creation.

However, Volf contests that Zizioulas's trinitarian doctrine is actually asymmetrical, in the sense that it is caused and maintained by the *monarchia* Father. Thus, perfect reciprocity among the persons in the Trinity is subject to doubt with respect of Zizioulas's insistence on *monarchia*. Volf reasons that Zizioulas actually wants a pre-determined, hierarchical church model, so he endorses it by constructing an asymmetrical Trinity. Volf has constructed a more equalitarian doctrine of the Trinity and church model. However, as explained in chapter 5, unlike Zizioulas, Volf does not systematically construct and present either his doctrine of the Trinity or the relation of the Trinity to the doctrine of creation. In his book *After His Likeness,* his goal is not to publish a systematic account of the Trinity. Rather, he constructs an ecclesiology for the Free Church through comparing the doctrines of the Trinity and ecclesiologies of Zizioulas and Ratzinger. In this book, Volf offers a perichoretic doctrine of the Trinity. He highlights that the three divine persons mutually constitute each other and embrace each other in love. The reciprocity between the three persons in giving and receiving each other, rather than demolishing their uniqueness, affirms each other. Volf endorses the perichoretic Trinity against Zizioulas's asymmetrical Trinity. First of all, Volf disagrees with Zizioulas that the numeric oneness is necessary in maintaining the unity of the Trinity. In Volf's thinking, the reciprocal love among the three persons sustains the unity. It is possible to envisage that Volf concurs with Nicholaos Loudivioks's comment that the otherness in the Trinity suggested by Zizioulas leads to "dictated

---

24. Zizioulas, *One and Many*, 15.

otherness."[25] One question remains on how such an asymmetrical doctrine of the Trinity, which forms the basis of the Eucharist in Zizioulas's system, can be correlated to the countering of individualism that basically declines reciprocal giving and receiving.

Unlike Zizioulas, Volf does not go into details of how the perichoretic Trinity participates in creation or *vice versa*. He does not specifically give a trinitarian narrative of God's creativity. He briefly mentions God and creation by emphasizing Genesis 1 as the narrative of God's pattern of creation that differentiates and binds the entities. Creatures are differentiated for interdependence, not exclusion. This interdependence can be understood as the reciprocity of the perichoretic Trinity extended to nature as a part of nature. Identity results from differentiation from the other and also the interiority of personal characteristics. As such, humanity is created and participates in the reciprocity of God as creatures, thus making them interdependent. Volf's suggestion that God created by differentiation for interdependence but not for exclusion forms the theological basis against the exclusive culture, which diminishes interdependence. Moreover, the idea that God's creation is not for exclusion can be understood as openness or inclusiveness to others. Volf understands and relates God's inclusiveness to the Eucharist, which is the divine embrace to all, perpetrators and victims alike. When the faithful participate in the Eucharist, the Creator God embraces them, excluding no one. In other words, the inclusive God is catholic, and human beings created by God are supposedly catholic too.

It can be seen from this discussion that Volf does not make a clear connection between the trinitarian narrative and creation as obviously as Zizioulas does, not even as it relates to the Eucharist. However, Volf connects the Trinity to grace (soteriological) with respect to the cross and the Eucharist in order to counter social exclusion. Volf's correlation in the soteriological aspect will be discussed later. Among these three theologians, de Lubac's connection between the Trinity and creation is the least clear with respect to the Eucharist. However, his arguments are more soteriological, because he argues that there is no complete demarcation between supernatural-natural, and that God communicates himself to human beings by grace.

---

25. Loudovikos, "Person instead of Grace," 692.

Soteriological Aspect (in the Order of Grace)

Based on his understanding of Aquinas, that "Grace is viewed as the self-communication of God to human person with the intent to transform that person: grace building nature,"[26] de Lubac insists on the interaction between nature and the supernatural through grace. He corrects what was in his day the neo-Thomist misreading of Aquinas by re-asserting the participation of supernatural in the natural. With this correction, de Lubac is able to interpret sacraments as mediatory between the supernatural and the natural. Put differently, the sacraments mediate grace to build human beings. Based on the sacramental mediation of grace, the Eucharist mediates or communicates grace to transform the participants. De Lubac also emphasizes that the Eucharist, as the sacrament of unity, unifies the faithful in Christ. He contests that in the Eucharist " . . .does each individual receive such grace in proportion as he is joined, socially, to that one body whence flows the saving life-stream."[27] Thus, the unity in Christ in the Eucharist is crucial for the formation of the spirit of Catholicism in resisting the individualistic piety of the faithful when they participate in the Liturgy.

Though de Lubac asserts the interaction between nature and the supernatural and the importance of mediation between them, he is not specific in formulating a trinitarian narrative of this interaction and thus does not weave it to the Eucharist. For this reason, Wood comments that in de Lubac's model the source of unity among human beings is more christocentric than trinitarian.[28] Being more critical than Wood, McPartlan criticizes that although de Lubac intends there to be social connection among the faithful when they are unified in Christ through the Eucharist, he fails to explain how to address the differences among them. It is not just the unity that matters in countering individualism. What also matters is the theological understanding of differences. The individualistic culture, after all, stems from self-centered ways to handle differences.

Due to this lack of a trinitarian source of unity and of the account of interpreting difference or otherness, de Lubac is faced with the challenge of proving the validity of his interpretation of the Eucharist in countering individualism. While de Lubac fails to clearly account for how Christians

---

26. Pivarnik, *Trinitarian Theology*, 3.

27. De Lubac, *Catholicism*, 48.

28. Wood, *Spiritual Exegesis*, 133.

are brought into "completion by means of one another"[29] in the Eucharist, Zizioulas offers a more thorough account that is based on the Trinity.

Zizioulas explains that the primordial communion of the three divine persons in the Trinity saves humanity from the individualistic cultural current. He gives a trinitarian narrative that bestows salvific grace to humanity in order to transform human beings so that they can resist the individualistic culture. Zizioulas claims that based on the unifying *monarchia* in the patristic teachings, the primordial communion of the three divine persons generates and sanctifies otherness without jeopardizing it. The three persons remain in communion without compromising their difference and uniqueness. He further explains how the connection of the Trinity and the Eucharist can save human beings from individualism. The Eucharist is the communion of the Trinity in which otherness is not separation (*diairesis*); it affirms otherness in the communion. Arguing that the Eucharist is the most anti-individualistic act of the church, Zizioulas maintains that the Liturgy offers a eucharistic *ethos* of otherness which stems from the communion of otherness in the Trinity. As such, when the faithful participate in the Eucharist, they participate in the communion of the otherness of the trinitarian God, and they are transformed by grace to live the *ethos* of otherness.

It is just to say that Zizioulas offers more theological clarity than de Lubac in his interpretation of differences in light of the Trinity and connects it to resist individualism through participation in the Eucharist. De Lubac focuses predominantly on unity in Christ and pays less theological attention to difference. However, as seen earlier, Zizioulas's subscription to *monarchia* holding the unity of the Trinity may discount the countering power of the Eucharist to the individualistic culture that he intends it to have. It has already been mentioned that both Volf and Loudovikos have challenged him on this point.

In addition to offering a trinitarian interpretation of the Eucharist to counter individualism, Zizioulas, also based on the doctrine of the Trinity, addresses soteriologically the ecological crisis. Unlike de Lubac's ambiguous stance on the inclusion or non-inclusion of creation in nature, Zizioulas is unequivocal on this point. He explicates that the desire of the triune God to have communion with the whole cosmos by recapitulation through his Son is exactly what Incarnation is all about. Based on the teachings of St. Maximus the Confessor, Zizioulas explains that Christ is the primordial

29. De Lubac, *Catholicism*, 184.

priest of creation, who redeems and then presents the whole creation to God. The church, which is the Mystical Body of Christ, is entrusted with the same task of continuing this priesthood in the Eucharist and daily life outside the Liturgy. By invoking the Holy Spirit in the Eucharist, the bishop together with the laity, acts as the priest of creation to offer themselves and also the material world for sanctification and acceptance by the triune God. When the faithful participate in the Eucharist, they are also transformed into the priest of creation by the trinitarian God, who participates in recapitulating the whole world through them.

Compared to de Lubac, Zizioulas expresses a more explicit cosmological intention in the Eucharist. He correlates the Eucharist to the trinitarian communion, who desires the whole world to be saved and recapitulated. However, Volf can remain critical of Zizioulas by insisting on his query about the asymmetrical trinitarian communion, which may cast doubts on whether human beings can really be the priest of creation and have perfect communion with the material world. Volf contests that the asymmetrical Trinity maintained by Zizioulas actually impedes the reciprocity between humanity and nature, and thus renders Zizioulas's countering of the exploitive culture on environment not as valid as he intends it to be. This is because dictated otherness may not be imposed on human beings alone but also on the material world.

In the soteriological aspect, Volf connects the Eucharist to the Trinity on the cross, when he counters the exclusive culture with the Eucharist. The Eucharist is the re-enactment of the divine embrace extended from the perichoretic love of the Trinity to the cross. In the Eucharist, the participants commemorate the memory of the Passion and are transformed by the triune God to become catholic personalities to live a life of embrace to counter social exclusion. The memory of the Passion re-enacted in the Eucharist entails the outpouring of the perichoretic love of the Trinity from the cross to humanity. Participants in the Eucharist, perpetrators and victims alike, are embraced and transformed by the perichoretic love of the triune God to imitate God's self-giving in a creaturely way. Volf argues that correspondence between the embrace at the divine level and the human level can only be analogous, because there is no complete interiority in human beings. In a nutshell, Volf suggests a soteriology based on the perichoretic model of the Trinity that predicates the social engagement of the faithful to counter the exclusive culture. And this soteriology is vivified in the Eucharist. As such, Volf offers a countercultural interpretation of the Eucharist that resists social exclusion in the larger society.

It is certain that Zizioulas criticizes Volf's proposal of the perichoretic Trinity inasmuch as Volf is suspicious of Zizioulas's *monarchia* Trinity participating in the Eucharist. On one hand, Zizioulas criticizes Volf, maintaining that the rejection of *monarchia* Father is a grave departure from the patristic teachings and traditions that both give life to the church, in order to embody the one-and-the-many of the Trinity, and shape to the episcopal-centric church model. On the other hand, Volf has already challenged Zizioulas's hierarchical Trinity as actually being an endorsement to a pre-determined hierarchical church model. Yet, Zizioulas can challenge Volf in a similar way: Is it true that Volf wants to construct a more egalitarian ecclesiology for the Free Church? If the answer were positive, would it be possible for Volf to propose a pre-determined egalitarian church model by endorsing the perichoretic Trinity? Furthermore, would Volf's "polycentric-participative" church model be understood by Zizioulas as "communitarian" ecclesiology,[30] especially in light of Volf's position that the ordained offices should be regarded merely as *bene esse* of the ecclesial community? Amidst the disagreement between Volf and Zizioulas, would de Lubac's complementarity of "the Eucharist makes the Church" and "the Church produces the Eucharist" be a useful means of avoiding over-hierarchical ecclesiology, which may dampen the communion of believers with God and with one another? All these possible questions lead to the comparative evaluation of the trinitarian participation in the Eucharist from the ecclesiological aspect, and how such participation relates to the countering of cultural currents by the Eucharist.

Ecclesiological Aspect (in the Order of Communion)

It is true that the trinitarian narrative in de Lubac's interpretation of the Eucharist is not as evident as in the interpretations of Zizioulas and Volf. However, it is still instructive to examine how he interprets the Eucharist as the communion of the faithful, with God and with one another, to counter both the hierarchical and totalitarian cultural currents. First and foremost, de Lubac re-emphasizes the ecclesial realism in order to correct the undue attention to the eucharistic realism. Basically, he asserts that though the church produces the Eucharist, the Eucharist is for all. He actually puts

30. Volf, *After Our Likeness*, 227.

a check on the growing institutional power of the church of his time. At the same time, he reminds the faithful of their general priesthood. On equal footing with sanctity, they should participate in the Eucharist and the communion with God together with the bishop, who has the ministerial priesthood. This ministerial priesthood or hierarchical power, should not be understood by itself, but "via the action by which this function is carried out,"[31] meaning the consecration of the bread and wine for the whole church. De Lubac gives equal stress to the ministerial priesthood of the bishop in exercising *persona* Christ and the complementarity of "the Church produces the Eucharist" and "the Eucharist produces the Church." By doing so, he actually gives the ecclesial reality of the participation of the faithful. First, the participation of the faithful in the Eucharist, or God's communion, is predominantly christological. Second, the communion of the faithful in God should not be hierarchical. The office of bishop is mediatory, but not intermediary between God and Christians. In other words, de Lubac argues that, through the Eucharist, this nonhierarchical communion of all the faithful in God encourages and strengthens the participants to resist not just the individualistic cultural current, but also the hierarchical and totalitarian cultures. However, while de Lubac's correlation of the Eucharist with the countering of the totalitarian cultural current sounds valid ecclesiologically, his interpretation fails to stimulate his church to be more self-critical. The fact is that the ecclesiastical polity may not always be influenced by theologians' discourses.

In stark contrast to de Lubac, Zizioulas insists that based on the *monarchia* of the Cappadocian Fathers, the communion of the church is ontologically hierarchical. *Taxis* or order is necessary to church structure and the Eucharist, insofar as they are consistent with the asymmetrical Trinity participating in the church and the Liturgy. As long as the hierarchy of the church and the structure of the Liturgy engender and affirm otherness in a way consistent with the trinitarian existence, they should remain the way they are. Based on the hierarchical Trinitarian existence, Zizioulas gives theological grounds for the four-layer structure of the church: bishop, priest, deacon, and laity. This hierarchy of the church is at its summit in the Eucharist. The Liturgy is episcopal-centric, in which the bishop is *alter Christus* and *alter apostolus*, vivifying the unity of the church with the Trinity. In particular, Zizioulas stresses that the presence of laity and their response of amen is a necessity in the Eucharist. Therefore, he may question

31. De Lubac, *Splendor*, 149.

why de Lubac allows a private mass in which a solo monk is sufficient.[32] Zizioulas may also argue that such a private mass with no laity involved would be a self-defeating act, since it undermines what de Lubac claims about the unifying role of the Eucharist in countering the individualistic culture.

Since de Lubac lived much earlier than Zizioulas, he could not give a rebuttal regarding this possible challenge from the Metropolitan. Yet a conjecture can be made here based on the background of de Lubac's theological career. Being the prominent figure of the New Theology movement, de Lubac immersed himself in re-reading patristic studies and re-engaging the church with these teachings in order to promote liturgical renewal.[33] Because he is so familiar with the works of the Fathers, de Lubac is quick to point out that Zizioulas's single-mindedness in endorsing the Cappadocian teaching of *monarchia* concerning the conception of the hierarchical communion and church structure needs further clarification. Zizioulas would need to support his endorsement of the Cappadocian Fathers' concept of "'cause' into the being of God assumed an incalculable importance"[34] over other views, when in fact there is a spectrum of patristic visions regarding the being of God. Given there is such a spectrum, what is Zizioulas's point of reference regarding the "incalculable importance" when he asserts that the notion of *monarchia* is typically patristic and well taken?[35] Why is the mutual causality of the three persons not considered? Furthermore, the cause is not necessarily greater than the effect. Therefore, though Zizioulas argues that the Father causes the Son, the Father is not necessarily greater than the Son. As such, the Trinity does not need to be asymmetrical, as Zizioulas contests. Moreover, since Zizioulas's argument for full reciprocity in the doctrine of the Trinity is in doubt, the validity of his interpretation of the Eucharist as the *ethos* of otherness to counter the individualistic culture is subject to query.

In comparison with de Lubac, Volf goes farther in advocating an egalitarian communion of believers based on the perichoretic Trinity model,

---

32. Ibid., 151.

33. Wood, "Henri de Lubac," 319.

34. Zizioulas, *Being as Communion*, 17.

35. Torrance, *Persons in Communion*, 293–94. For example, as noted by Alan J. Torrance, there are different patristic visions of the being of God: Gregory Nazianzen's concept of a Trinity of hypostatic relations, Athanasius's doctrine of the reciprocal indwelling of the three hypostases, and Cyril of Alexandria's idea of the procession of the Spirit from the Father through the Son.

which is more acceptable to the Free Church. Whereas de Lubac points out the need to maintain the equality of ministerial priesthood and general priesthood in order to restrain the over-institutionalized church from becoming totalitarian, Volf recalls Luther's recovery of the participative model of ecclesial life based on the "universal priesthood of believers"[36] to support the egalitarian relationship in the church. More importantly, Volf employs the perichoretic trinitarian model to give the theological framework for his ecclesiological communion, which is reciprocal and participative. His egalitarian communion of the church, analogous to the perichoretic Trinity, is in stark contrast to Zizioulas's bipolar communion. Volf's criticism of this bipolarity is that the bishop acts while the congregation only receives.[37] Arguing that ordained offices are *bene esse* and provisional only, Volf does not subscribe to the unifying and mediatory role of the bishop according to de Lubac, much less Zizioulas's overarching emphasis on the centrality of the bishop in the Eucharist. Volf's position on the ordained offices and emphasis on the laity's participation leaves him open to the accusation of being communitarian, in points of both the Eucharist and communion of the ecclesial body. This is a position that neither de Lubac nor Zizioulas would abide. Moreover, this position seems to be especially untenable, since Volf regards the bishop, or priest, or simply the ordained office-holder as not acting *in persona Christi* according to his proposal of the egalitarian and participative model of communion. However, Volf can defend himself against the charge of being communitarian by his insistence that the sacraments are *esse* of the church.[38] If Volf, like some evangelicals, considered the Eucharist as *bene esse* of the church (an ordinance of God regulating the common life of Christians), the Eucharist would not be a sacrament that ushers them into participation in the life of the Trinity.[39] There would not be anything to be mediated by it and nothing to cause the participants to really participate in the triune God. However, it is not the participation of the laity that effectuates the Eucharist; it is the Eucharist as the *esse* of the church that really counts. Volf's emphasis on the Eucharist as *esse* of the church is important to his interpretation of the Eucharist as the re-enactment of the perichoretic love of the Trinity flowing to the cross to

36. Volf, *After Our Likeness*, 166, 225.

37. Ibid., 224.

38. Volf, *After Our Likeness*, 152–53.

39. Boersma, *Heavenly Participation*, 105.

transform the participants to be catholic agents. This transformation in the Eucharist empowers the communion of the church to be inclusive.

Insofar as Volf maintains the perichoretic trinitarian model and its connection to the Eucharist, he is able to give an inclusive shape to the communion of the church to counter the exclusive culture. The correlation between his theological interpretation of the Eucharist and the communion of the church to ward off social exclusion remains valid. However, as mentioned earlier, Volf's theology is not characteristically eucharistic. He has borrowed traditions from the Catholic Church and the Orthodox Church to relate the Eucharist to catholic personality.[40] Probably de Lubac and Zizioulas would ask Volf the following questions: what precise liturgy or ritual can Volf offer to effectively mediate the transformation of the lives of participants that would counter social exclusion? What would be the shape of the Liturgy of the Eucharist in Volf's Free Church ecclesiology for enhancing such mediation? In fact, the query of effectiveness is equally applicable for all three theologians, because the transformation of participants to engage in countering cultural currents is not just about the validity of theological interpretation or catechesis, but also ritual-liturgical effectiveness.[41] As noted by Kevin Irwin, *lex vivendi* (the life in relation to liturgy) has to be related to *lex agendi* (the way in which the liturgy is performed).[42] While the validity of the Eucharist in countering cultural currents is assessed by the theological concepts, the effectiveness of liturgy, *lex vivendi,* demands not just the theological interpretation but also the method of enacting the liturgical-ritual (*lex agendi*).

EFFECTIVENESS IN COUNTERING CULTURAL CURRENTS

This book mainly focuses on how de Lubac, Zizioulas, and Volf correlate the theological interpretations of the Eucharist to cultural currents. Yet, it is worthwhile to examine briefly whether and how they describe the liturgical activities of the Eucharist to form the participants to counter cultural currents in their daily lives. How effectively can this description of the Eucharist nurture the participants to become countercultural? Such effectiveness hinges upon how well *opus operatum* (the objective act of the liturgy)

40. Volf, *Exclusion and Embrace*, 129.

41. Pivarnik, *Trinitarian Theology*, 2.

42. Irwin, *Context and Text*, 55–56.

can stimulate *opus operans* (the disposition of the participants).[43] Below is an examination of the ritual-liturgical aspect of their descriptions of the Eucharist.

Among the three theologians, Volf's description is the least clear concerning the concrete form of the liturgical action of the Eucharist. He does not mention the ritual-liturgical aspect of the Eucharist in relation to countering exclusion. Though he correlates the Eucharist to the divine embrace of the Trinity to counter social exclusion, Volf offers no liturgical details to substantiate how his interpretation can impress the participants with the disposition of embrace. His tradition fails to demonstrate the trinitarian participation in liturgical texts, prayers, hymns, and descriptions of actions of both the clergy and the laity in the Eucharist, be it Protestant or Free Church. Interestingly, once again in his book *Exclusion and Embrace*, Volf has borrowed the Orthodox resources, a hymn this time, which can better illustrate how the Eucharist is the divine embrace to counter the exclusive cultural current by urging joyful mutual embrace among the faithful.[44]

Since Volf does not furnish his description and explanation of how the liturgical performance of the Eucharist can empower the participants to become catholic personalities able to resist social exclusion, the effectiveness of his proposal in the order of ritual-liturgical is unascertained. The lack of ritual-liturgical specificity and thus effectiveness may be due to Volf's proposal of the Free Church ecclesiology, which is malleable as far as liturgy is concerned. More importantly, de Lubac and Zizioulas can challenge Volf concerning his stance on the open commensality of the Eucharist: is the Liturgy open for all? He is quiet on whether the Eucharist is exclusive to the baptized. If so, how would the liturgical action of the Eucharist mediate grace to transform the participants to embrace others when it excludes the non-baptized? As far as effectiveness in the ritual-liturgical aspect is concerned, Volf's account of participation in the Eucharist to produce catholic agents to counter social exclusion is not promising. However, his challenge to the hierarchical structure of the Eucharist, especially the bipolarity between the bishop and the laity, should attract attention to the laity's passivity in the Liturgy.

Like Volf, de Lubac does not give a description of the liturgical actions, texts, and prayers of the Eucharist to explain how it can empower the participants to live a life contrary to the individualistic and totalitarian

43. Pivarnik, *Trinitarian Theology*, 149.

44. Volf, *Exclusion and Embrace*, 130.

cultural currents. However, he recalls the teachings of the Council of Trent to reflect how the Eucharist produces the fruit of unity:

> It was the will of Christ to make of this sacrament the symbol of that Body of which he is himself the Head, to which he would bind us as his members by the close bonds of faith, hope and charity, so that all should be but one reality, with never a division.[45]

De Lubac also quotes Augustine's homily to explain to the newly baptized their participation in the bread and wine in the Eucharist:

> We shall say nothing of our own about it, rather let us hear the Apostle, who speaking of this sacrament says: "We being many are one body, one bread." Understand and rejoice. Unity, devotion, charity! One bread: and what is this one bread? One body made up of many. Consider that the bread is not made of one grain alone, but of many . . . . At baptism you were wetted with water. Then the Holy Spirit came into you like the fire which bakes the dough. Be then what you see and receive what you are.
>
> Now for the Chalice, my brethren, remember how wine is made. Many grapes hang on the bunch, but the liquid which runs out of them mingles together in unity. So has the Lord willed that we should belong to him and he has consecrated on his altar the mystery of our peace and our unity.[46]

Though de Lubac does not explain how the ritual-liturgical aspect of the Eucharist supports his theological agenda of resisting the individualistic cultural current, he goes further than Volf to show how the Fathers have commented on the scriptural and liturgical texts regarding the unifying function of the Eucharist.[47] He clearly demonstrates his attention to the liturgical texts and prayers in terms of how they support unity as a fruit of the Eucharist for countering individualism. For example, he mentions the ancient Armenian liturgy, the liturgical prayer of St. Eustace, and the *anaphora* of the "Apostolic Constitutions."[48] Though de Lubac does not offer a thorough description to demonstrate how the liturgical action, texts

---

45. De Lubac, *Catholicism*, 52.

46. *Sermons* 272 and 234 (P.L. xxxviii, 1247 and 1116), quoted in de Lubac, *Catholicism*, 53.

47. De Lubac, *Catholicism*, 49–54. De Lubac quotes the teachings of Irenaeus, the inscription on the baptistery of the Lateran, St. Cyprian, St. John Chrysostom, and St. Cyril of Alexandria respectively to highlight his attention to the liturgical teachings or texts on the Eucharist.

48. Ibid., 61.

and prayers can counter individualism, his use of these liturgical texts and prayers show that he has a better awareness than Volf does regarding the importance of the ritual-liturgical aspect of the Eucharist in countering cultural currents. However, de Lubac does not mention anything about the liturgical activity of the Eucharist in countering totalitarian culture. Therefore, it is difficult to comment on the liturgical-ritual effectiveness of his interpretation of the Eucharist for this purpose. Though de Lubac argues for the equality of the ministerial priesthood of the bishop and the general priesthood of the laity, practically speaking, the growing hierarchical and totalitarian culture of the church has caused the passivity of the laity in the Eucharist. It is helpful to point out that the significance of the active and fruitful participation of the laity is not an issue until *Sacrosanctum Concilium* (December 4, 1963). Though de Lubac is not specific enough in describing and explaining how the ritual-liturgical aspect of the Eucharist can counter hierarchical and totalitarian cultural currents, he is prophetic in pointing out this potential, which is later addressed by the Catholic Church.

Compared to Volf and de Lubac, Zizioulas offers a more concrete description of how the Eucharist can stimulate the faithful to live a lifestyle countering the exploitive cultural trend on creation. In *The Eucharistic Communion and the World*, Zizioulas describes how the actions and prayers of the Eucharist embody the utmost active acceptance of the world and creation in the Orthodox tradition:

> All the faithful who go to the liturgy bring the world with them (and we mean it in the most realistic way). They bring not merely human flesh, concrete human beings with its weaknesses and passions. They bring their relations with the natural world, with creation. In the ancient Church (but also today in the places where simple traditional piety has not yet been completely ousted by intellectual dissociation), the faithful not only went to church, but they brought with them gifts of creation: bread, wine and oil. And these gifts were carried in liturgical procession (on parade) to arrive in the hands of the Bishop who was waiting at the entrance (the current 'Grand Entrance' of the Liturgy) and who would offer them to God as Eucharist . . . the Liturgy requires the faithful to make their contribution and to pray for 'mild weather, abundant fruits of the earth . . .'[49]

49. Ibid., 125.

In the Eucharist, the bishop makes the *anaphora* with the presence of the laity to realize their priesthood of creation. Zizioulas shows that the physical movements of the laity, the liturgical dynamics between the bishop and the laity, and also the *anaphora* prayers give the participants the liturgical experience of a eucharistic worldview: the material world should be recapitulated in communion with God through the priest of creation. Zizioulas adds that "Bringing the world as it is with them, the faithful receive a foretaste of paradise, an eschatological glimpse of the world as it will be, and then are called again to 'go in peace' back into the world."[50] Compared with Volf and de Lubac, Zizioulas is more specific in describing how the ritual aspect of the Eucharist is effective in transforming the faithful to counter cultural currents through their participation in the Liturgy. However, according to the structure of the eucharistic assembly that Zizioulas insists on, it is difficult to ascertain how effective the Eucharist can be in countering individualism. According to Zizioulas, the liturgy of the Eucharist is highly structured and hierarchical. The bishop is at the center of the Eucharist and is surrounded by priests, deacons, and laity to exemplify the one-and-the-many of the trinitarian God. Volf has questioned Zizioulas concerning how this asymmetrical structure can be theologically conducive to reciprocity, which is crucial in countering individualism. From the perspective of ritual-liturgical, the laity may feel this asymmetry more visually and physically, than intellectually. If the participants in the Liturgy do not feel the mutual reciprocity, how can they be transformed to live the *ethos* of otherness and be reciprocal to others in their daily lives? Thus, the Eucharist is not ritually effective in countering the individualistic culture as Zizioulas claims.

SUMMARY

This comparative evaluation examines how personal and theological backgrounds, as well as time and place in which the theologians live, impact their cultural awareness and their interpretations of the cultural currents, which they identify as contrary to Christian values. Regarding the correlation of the Eucharist with cultural currents, the doctrine of the Trinity is adopted as a common plane for comparison in three aspects: metaphysical, soteriological, and ecclesiological respectively.

In respect of the metaphysical aspect, among the three, de Lubac is the least clear in relating the Trinity to creation and the Eucharist, probably due

50. Ibid.

to his lack of a cosmological intention in his interpretation of the Eucharist. Zizioulas shows the greatest clarity in relating the doctrine of Trinity by resorting to *monarchia* as the cause of creation. He also argues that the communion of the divine persons maintained by *monarchia* forms the basis of the Eucharist for being the communion of otherness to counter individualism. Though Volf does not really emphasize the cosmological dimension of the Eucharist, he contests that the perichoretic Trinity gives the reciprocity of creation, which is an important theological ground opposing the cultural current of social exclusion, which violates the embracing love of the Creator God.

As far as the soteriological aspect is concerned, de Lubac reiterates that the Eucharist is a sacrament of unity that mediates grace to save humanity. Yet the connection he makes in order to relate the trinitarian doctrine to the Eucharist in this aspect is not as vivid as Zizioulas and Volf. Zizioulas, however, by resorting again to *monarchia,* which sustains the unity, clearly connects the trinitarian participation in the Eucharist to counter individualism. He also addresses the ecological crisis by adopting the patristic concept of the priest of creation in the Eucharist and the recapitulation of creation to the Trinity. As for Volf, he is consistent in using the perichoretic doctrine of the Trinity as a social model to counter social exclusion by connecting the perichoretic love flowing from the cross to the re-enactment of the memory of the Passion in the Eucharist.

Regarding the ecclesiological aspect, though de Lubac's suggestion that the mutuality of "the Church produces the Eucharist" and "the Eucharist produces the Church" helps the church counter hierarchical and totalitarian cultural currents, he does not make an obvious connection between this mutuality and the doctrine of the Trinity. While Zizioulas is unequivocal in maintaining that the *monarchia* of the Trinity supports both the episcopal-centric structure of the church and the Eucharist, Volf affirmatively states that an egalitarian and poly-participative church model and the Eucharist are supported by the perichoretic doctrine of the Trinity.

Finally, the effectiveness of the ritual-liturgical activity in countering cultural currents by the Eucharist, according to their interpretations and traditions, is assessed. Among the three, Volf does not give any description or explanation of the liturgical activity from his Protestant tradition. Thus the effectiveness of his interpretation of the Eucharist to counter the current of social exclusion is subject to query. Compared with Volf, de Lubac shows more awareness of the importance of liturgical activity in countering individualism by referring to the relevant teachings of church councils and the Fathers. Yet he fails to mention liturgical details to elucidate the effectiveness of his interpretation of the Liturgy. Only Zizioulas offers the description of liturgical activity of the Eucharist in the Orthodox Church to illustrate how the cosmological intention is vivified in the eucharistic assembly to nurture the faithful to care for creation.

7

Conclusion

THIS RESEARCH ARGUES THAT the Eucharist can be studied as a countercultural liturgy. The term countercultural here refers to the upholding of identity and values of the Christian community by countering cultural currents that are contrary to the Christian faith. The reason for supporting this argument is three-fold. First, the historical studies of the Eucharist show that this liturgy has been countercultural ever since it was conceived in the early Christian communities. The empirical experience of the early Christian communities with the Eucharist testified to its countercultural function against the prevailing cultural trends in Greco-Roman society. Second, the general theory of ritual explains how the Eucharist, as a ritual, can actually assert the difference between the realm of ritual and the real world. This reinforced difference forms schemes leading to countercultural behaviors *vis-á-vis* the mainstream culture in the real world. Thus, the Eucharist can be regarded as a ritualization process to inculcate participants to be agents to resist cultural currents. Third, the discussion of the theology of culture also shows that liturgy can have a countercultural function. Liturgy can be pedagogical in priming the love and attention of human beings toward a desired way of life through their physical involvement in the liturgy. As such, the Eucharist can be pedagogical in nurturing the participants to live a life consistent with Christian identity and values in a society that may advocate differently. These three reasons demonstrate that the study of the Eucharist as a countercultural liturgy is historically, ritually, and theologically grounded.

It has also been pointed out that, up to date, there has not been any comparative study of the countercultural function of the Eucharist across different church traditions. This study has attempted to fill this research gap by examining the theological interpretations of the Eucharist offered by de Lubac, Zizioulas and Volf, who represent the Catholic, Orthodox, and Protestant traditions respectively. Below is the summary of the findings of the comparison between these three theologians regarding their interpretations of the countercultural function of the Eucharist.

In de Lubac's treatment, the cultural significance of the Eucharist lies in its mediatory role. It mediates the supernatural to the natural, including the cultural world. Moreover, the Eucharist, as the sacrament of unity, is fundamentally important in de Lubac's programmatic concept of Catholicism, which is a top priority of his theological agenda. He is concerned with the individualistic culture as well as the totalitarian and the hierarchical cultural currents. De Lubac goes into more detail than the other two concerning how the Eucharist can counter individualism. However, he fails to explain how the Eucharist can handle otherness or difference, both of which are core concerns when considering individualistic culture. In addition, his interpretation of the Eucharist to counter the totalitarian and the hierarchical cultures is not as valid as he intended, because when he lived the Catholic Church had been deemed as totalitarian and hierarchical for centuries. What is theologically sound still has to meet the resistance from church culture and polity.

The centrality of the Eucharist in Zizioulas's theology is indisputable. The patristic teachings concerning the doctrine of the Trinity have greatly influenced his interpretation of the Eucharist and ecclesiology. Both the Eucharist and the structure of the church should embody the asymmetric trinitarian existence, namely, *monarchia*, which is represented by the presidency of the bishop. Zizioulas identifies the exploitive culture toward creation and individualism. Though Zizioulas stresses that the Eucharist is the affirmation and acceptance of otherness to counter individualism, he still insists on the *monarchia* of the Trinity, which is asymmetric. Therefore, doubt remains as to the validity of his interpretation, because such an asymmetric relationship impedes reciprocal self-giving and does not help counter individualism. To resist the exploitive culture toward environment, which causes ecological crisis, Zizioulas employs the notion of the priest of creation in the patristic teachings and emphasizes the cosmological intention of the Eucharist, which points to the recapitulation of the whole creation to God. However, Zizioulas needs to further explain theologically how the liturgical experience can influence the behaviors of the faithful outside the Eucharist in order to counter the exploitive culture on creation. Because the monarchical model of the immanent Trinity advocated by Zizioulas brings forth a monarchical model of God-world relationship, this asymmetric model may imply the dictated otherness as it relates to the environment. Though such dictated otherness does not necessarily infer an exploitative attitude toward the environment, it may look less environmentally friendly than the organic model of God-world relationship. If this is the case, Zizioulas's monarchical model is not so effective in countering the cultural trends of exploitative attitude toward nature. In other words, the monarchical model is not very convincing with regard to the ecological crisis.

Among the three, Volf's theology is the least eucharistic. Though he regards baptism and the Eucharist as *esse* of the church, his ecclesiology is not based on the theology of the Eucharist; in fact he has not constructed one. To counter social exclusion, he constructs the theology of embrace by elaborating the Eucharist as the sacrament of the embrace of God, which is actually the ecumenical understanding of the Liturgy. Moreover, he had to borrow from the Catholic and Orthodox traditions of catholic personality to connect the Eucharist to countering the exclusive culture. Comparatively speaking, the position of the Eucharist in Volf's theology is not as clear as in the other two theologians' systems. Furthermore, Volf obviously needs resources from the Catholic and Orthodox traditions to buttress how, from the liturgical-ritual point of view, the Eucharist can help shape the catholic personality to resist social exclusion. Practically speaking, Volf mentions no description of liturgical details of the Eucharist. However, the analytical clarity of Volf in cultural analysis excels de Lubac and Zizioulas. His multifaceted analysis of social exclusion and its impact on not only the church, but also society, demonstrates that of the three, Volf has the strongest sense of counterculture as far as the thoroughness of his cultural analysis is concerned.

These three theologians' interpretations of the Eucharist reveal that they all recognize the countercultural function of the Eucharist, though the validity varies in their interpretations of the Eucharist in relation to countering cultural trends. A comparative evaluation of their efforts in explicating the countercultural function of the Eucharist according to their own traditions is conducted around the following four aspects: awareness of cultural currents, diagnosis of cultural currents, correlation of the Eucharist to cultural currents, and effectiveness of the Eucharist in countering cultural currents.

The personal backgrounds, theological traditions, and the particular context of the theologians have an integral impact on their awareness of cultural currents. By examining the attention de Lubac, Zizioulas, and Volf paid to different cultural currents this integral influence is clearly revealed. Within the ecumenical circle, Zizioulas has been discoursing on the ecological crisis since the early days of his theological career. He also pinpoints individualism, which is closely related to the abusive cultural current toward nature, which causes ecological crisis. He highlights that both cultural currents reflect the anthropocentric attitude of human beings. Though de Lubac also notes individualism, he devotes relatively more effort to explaining the totalitarian and hierarchical culture. Obviously, the totalitarian regimes and atheism that prevailed in his day pressured him to respond to them directly. De Lubac regards it is the responsibility of theologians and the church to candidly respond to these pressing cultural currents. Volf, a Croatian who witnessed genocide in Europe, is deeply affected by his personal experiences of being marginalized or excluded. That is why he is aware of social exclusion and why he advocates an egalitarian ecclesial model.

Regarding the diagnosis of cultural currents, only Volf can provide a multifaceted analysis from biblical, theological, and socio-cultural perspectives. De Lubac gives little analytical details in explaining the individualistic culture. He seems to presume that people are generally aware of this. Comparatively speaking, he devotes more effort to explicating the totalitarian cultural current in his context. While Zizioulas does not really propose a socio-cultural analysis of individualism and the exploitive impact of the cultural current on nature, he furnishes a theological exposition of these two cultural currents by using the patristic teachings on communion of divine persons of the Trinity and the notion of priest of creation.

The complexity of a comparative evaluation of the theologians' correlation of the Eucharist to cultural currents requires a common plane to make the assessment more structured and comprehensible. Since the Eucharist is inseparable from the Trinity, the interpretation of the trinitarian participation in the Eucharist and the participation of the faithful in the Trinity through the Eucharist are employed as a common axis for comparative assessment. The comparative evaluation is developed according to three aspects: metaphysical, soteriological, and ecclesiological. The validity of their correlations of the Eucharist to cultural currents is assessed in these three areas, adopting the trinitarian participation as a common basis of comparison.

Concerning the metaphysical aspect, Zizioulas connects more explicitly the doctrine of Trinity to creation and the Eucharist than the other two. He maintains that the Father is the *monarchia* who causes the Son and the Spirit to be, while humanity is created by the triune God through hypostasization in Christ through the power of the Holy Spirit. Zizioulas contests that the Eucharist is the highest point of the trinitarian communion. When the faithful participate in the Eucharist, they partake of the communion of otherness in the Trinity, which is Zizioulas's most important theological ground in correlating the Eucharist to counter individualism and the exploitive culture on creation. However, it is possible for both de Lubac and Volf to challenge Zizioulas's adherence to the *monarchia* of the Trinity, since the former is cautious of the hierarchical church structure and the latter advocates an egalitarian church model. Both Lubac and Volf could argue that Zizioulas's application of the asymmetric *monarchia* to the ecclesial structure actually makes the *ordo* of the church an "over-realized" trinitarian existence. Though Volf and de Lubac may post such a challenge, their connections of the doctrine of the Trinity and creation are not as evident as that of Zizioulas.

In the soteriological aspect, de Lubac is less specific than Zizioulas in connecting the doctrine of the Trinity to the Eucharist as far as salvation is concerned, albeit the former contests that the Eucharist mediates grace from the supernatural to the natural. In fact, de Lubac's interpretation of the Eucharist is more christocentric than trinitarian. Zizioulas applies the one-and-the-many of the Trinity, which is the communion of otherness, to the Eucharist to counter individualism and the exploitive culture toward creation. Yet, Zizioulas's communion of otherness faces Volf's challenge that such otherness is dictated or impressed by the *monarchia* so that it lacks full reciprocity in the communion. As such, it is subject to query whether or not Zizioulas's claim that through the Eucharist individualism and the exploitive culture that cause ecological crisis can be countered. As for Volf, he explains the Eucharist as the re-enactment of the divine embrace of the perichoretic Trinity on the cross, which transforms the participants to become catholic personalities to counter and heal social exclusion. However, as discussed previously, Volf himself acknowledges two challenges to mutual embrace between aggressors and victims: forgiveness and memories of wrongdoings.

Concerning the ecclesiological aspect, de Lubac does not weave the doctrine of the Trinity into the Eucharist as much as Zizioulas and Volf do. He rather focuses on advocating a nonhierarchical communion of believers in the Eucharist and re-emphasizing the mutuality of ecclesial realism and eucharistic realism. De Lubac argues that such nonhierarchical communion in the Eucharist empowers the participants to resist individualism, as well as the hierarchical and totalitarian culture. Zizioulas's commitment to the episcopal-centric church structure, as based on the monarchical Trinity, faces challenges, especially from Volf: that *monarchia* actually hinders reciprocal acceptance of otherness. *Monarchia*, in fact, discounts Zizioulas's effort to counter individualism by the celebration of the Eucharist. Since Volf is more concerned with the egalitarian church model, he advocates the perichoretic doctrine of the Trinity, which forms the theological ground of an egalitarian ecclesiology consistent with the Free Church tradition. He further argues that such an egalitarian ecclesial model facilitates the formation of catholic agents to live a life resisting social exclusion.

Regarding the aspect of the liturgical-ritual of the Eucharist, it is first necessary to take into account the different church traditions of these three theologians. Then a comparative assessment of the effectiveness of the Eucharist in nurturing the faithful to live out the sacramental-ethic in ordinary life is conducted. Volf's discussion, from this aspect, offers the least clarity, if any. His suggestion in forming catholic personality to counter social exclusion is not as promising as he intended, as far as the liturgical-ritual aspect is concerned. Comparatively speaking, de Lubac is able to make references to the relevant teachings of the Council of Trent and liturgical texts to support the unifying role of the Eucharist to counter individualism. He shows relatively more concrete understanding than Volf concerning the significance of the liturgical-ritual aspect of the Eucharist in countering cultural currents. By describing the liturgical details of the Orthodox Church, Zizioulas provides the richest ritual details among the three to substantiate his claim of the countercultural power of the Eucharist. However, none of them offer adequate details of the liturgical administration of the Eucharist in their respective traditions for an effective evaluation.

In addition to the above-mentioned comparative assessment, an overall evaluation of these three theologians is made in the following areas:

their common limitation, complementarity, and representation in their own tradition.

One common limitation of these three theologians is the lack of proof for the effectiveness of their interpretations of the Eucharist in countering cultural currents. Though their interpretations of the Eucharist show various extents of theological validity, the effectiveness of their interpretations to counter cultural currents needs further substantiation. This is probably due to the fact that they are systematic theologians who have no hesitation in demonstrating their attentiveness and astuteness to theological construction. However, they may not be keen on giving details of liturgical activities from the perspective of liturgists, who are involved on a practical level in administering the Eucharist and conveying its significance. As far as the practical aspect of the Eucharist is concerned, they do not offer details to illustrate how the ritual activities in their respective traditions can counter the cultural currents.

It is always a challenge to seek complementarity in a cross-church tradition study. This is especially true in this research since the Protestant tradition represented by Volf has a greater difference in heritage compared to the Catholic Church and the Orthodox Church. One important instance is the absence of a bishop in Volf's Free Church model (as proposed in his book *After His Likeness*). Such a difference makes the possibility to complement each other in the area of church order and the Eucharist particularly challenging. Yet, Zizioulas's idea of an ecclesial person who is a catholic mode of existence in the Eucharist is already a complement that supports Volf's notion of catholic personality, which is important to the theology of embrace to counter the exclusive culture. Moreover, though Volf does not resort to traditional Protestant resources to support his notion of catholic personality, Zizioulas's emphasis on acceptance and sanctification of otherness in the Eucharist can provide another avenue for Volf to further interpret how the catholic personality can be formed to embrace otherness in order to reproach social exclusion. Volf may also find the catholic mode of presence to otherness in the Eucharist a viable strategy in making cultural boundaries more permeable for the sake of countering social exclusion. However, a reinterpretation is needed before Volf could accept such a complementary use of Zizioulas's idea of acceptance of otherness in the Eucharist. To be consistent with his egalitarian ecclesiology, Volf would need to re-interpret Zizioulas's idea of otherness in order to make it more reciprocal in his perichoretic doctrine of the Trinity. Only then can he answer Nicholaos Loudovikos's query to Zizioulas concerning the dictated otherness allegedly caused by *monarchia*. In addition, Zizioulas's idea of affirmation of otherness in the Eucharist can also complement the lack of attention to the difference in de Lubac's discourse of unity in Christ through the Eucharist. This complementary use of Zizioulas's idea of otherness may buttress de Lubac's idea of "completion-by-means-of-each-other," which he actually leaves undeveloped. It also helps counter Paul McPartlan's challenge that de Lubac's concept of the unity in Christ through the Eucharist is just a "coincident unity-of-identity" that entails nothing to address difference, which is an important concern in countering individualism.

Zizioulas's overarching emphasis on the bishop as the icon of unity in the structure of the church and the Eucharist may risk the challenge of bipolarity, or the asymmetrical relationship between the bishop and the laity. However, de Lubac's complementarity of "the Church makes the Eucharist" and "the Eucharist is for all" helps guard against the two-tier sanctity of the bishop and the laity in the church. It can help Zizioulas reduce the possible drawbacks of the asymmetrical relationship between the bishop and the laity, which if not carefully checked, may become totalitarianism. While De Lubac's idea of equal sanctity in the bishop-laity relationship in the Eucharist and in the church structure can be a viable complement to Zizioulas's model of church order, it is difficult for Volf to be complementary to de Lubac and Zizioulas's theology of the Eucharist and ecclesiology. This is simply because Volf does not subscribe to episcopacy. This research shows that the break in tradition in the Protestant (or to be more exact, the Free Church ecclesial model suggested by him in *After His Likeness*) makes it difficult for Volf to be complementary to the other two theologians as far as the church structure is concerned.

Regarding the representation of these theologians in their own traditions with respect to their interpretations of the Eucharist, Zizioulas is shown as the one who is most representative of his Orthodox tradition. This evaluation is based on his adherence to the patristic tradition in interpreting the doctrine of the Trinity and connecting the Eucharist to countering the cultural currents identified by him. His subscription to the patristic teachings of *anaphora* and the priest of creation to address the exploitive impact of the cultural trend on nature, together with his development of the *ethos* of otherness to counter individualism, exemplify his firm allegiance to the Orthodox tradition.

Volf is found to be the least representative of the Protestant tradition. Though he claims that the Eucharist is important in forming the catholic personality, who is crucial in embodying the theology of embrace, he does not draw anything specifically from the Protestant tradition to apply to his interpretation of the Eucharist. Rather he admits that he has to seek teachings on the Eucharist from the Catholic and Orthodox repertoires. Furthermore, it is hard to ascertain Volf's representativeness because the Free Church model he has suggested actually encompasses a variation of traditions. It is difficult to ascertain how Volf is representative of this church tradition. He also does not mention any concrete ritual activity of the Eucharist to claim any allegiance to the Protestant or Free Church tradition. Thus, of the three, he is the least representative of his tradition.

De Lubac is positioned between Zizioulas and Volf in terms of his representation in his Catholic tradition. Compared with Zizioulas's allegiance to the Orthodox tradition, de Lubac's interpretation of the Eucharist and countering of the totalitarian and hierarchical cultural trends is not typical in the Catholic Church of his time. This is because he underscores that the Eucharist is for all, though the bishop has the prerogative to produce it. The bishop has no superiority over the laity in terms of sanctity or other aspects of life. His interpretation of the Eucharist is, in fact, a challenge to the totalitarian and hierarchical cultures of the Catholic Church. Therefore, it is just to say that de Lubac's interpretation of the Eucharist *vis-à-vis* the totalitarian and hierarchical cultural currents of the Catholic Church render him not representative of the tradition of his time, nor perhaps even now. However, de Lubac is representative of the Catholic tradition through his reiteration of the Eucharist as a sacrament of unity that joins all the faithful in Christ, along with the rejection of the Protestant idea of "subsidiary symbolism" of the Eucharist, which at its best, basically regards the Eucharist as communion of the faithful with some sort of mysterious presence of Christ. While it is true that de Lubac does not give as detailed a description of the ritual activity of the Eucharist as Zizioulas does, his citation of the teachings of councils and commentary on the liturgical texts partially reflects his adherence to the Catholic Church tradition. As such, in this comparative assessment of representation, de Lubac is posited between Zizioulas and Volf.

To conclude, this research affirms that the Eucharist can be studied as a countercultural liturgy and supports that it is open to different interpretations in order to counter different cultural currents by different church traditions. The Eucharist's openness to interpretation to counter different cultural currents is an instructive reminder to theologians of different traditions to further explore its countercultural potential. This research also demonstrates that a comparative study of this sort is necessary for conversation and mutual learning by remaining ecumenically open to each other's tradition. The vision of such a comparison is that different churches can be self-critical enough to strive to make the Eucharist a valid and effective liturgy to counter cultural currents, and by doing so, to affirm the identity and values of Christian communities.

Bibliography

Ables, Travis E. "On the Very Idea of an Ontology of Communion: Being, Relation and Freedom in Zizioulas and Levinas." *The Heythrop Journal* 52 (2011) 672–83.

Achtemeier, Paul J. "The Origin and Function of the Pre-Marcan Miracle Catenae." *Journal of Biblical Literature* 91 (1972) 198–221.

Arbuckle, Gerald A. *Culture, Inculturation, Theologians: A Postmodern Critique.* Collegeville: Liturgical, 2010.

Attridge, Harold W., ed. *The Apostolic Tradition.* Minneapolis: Fortress, 2002.

Au, Yik-pui. "The Eucharist as a Cultural Critique: A Construction Based on the Eucharistic Theology of John D. Zizioulas." *International Journal of Orthodox Theology* 3 (2012) 53–88.

———. "The Eucharist as a Countercultural Liturgy: An Examination of the Theology of Henri de Lubac (1896–1991)." *Sino-Christian Studies: An International Journal of Bible, Theology, & Philosophy* 19 (2015) 7–42.

Baeher, Peter, ed. *Hannah Arendt, Totalitarianism, and the Social Science.* Stanford: Stanford University Press, 2010.

Balthasar, Hans Urs von. *The Theology of Henri de Lubac: An Overview.* Translated by Joseph Fessio and Michael M. Waldstein. San Francisco: Ignatius, 1991.

Bell, Catherine. "Discourse and Dichotomies: The Structure of Ritual Theory." *Religion* 17 (1987) 95–118.

———. "The Ritual Body and the Dynamics of Ritual Power." *Journal of Ritual Study* 4 (1990) 299–313.

———. "Ritual, Change, and Changing Rituals." *Worship* 63 (1989) 31–41.

———. *Ritual: Perspectives and Dimensions.* New York: Oxford University Press, 1997.

———. *Ritual Theory, Ritual Practice.* New York: Oxford University Press, 1992.

Bellah, Robert Needly. "The Return of Religion: The Second Noble Lecture." *Religion and Intellectual Life* 1 (1984) 40–56.

Bevans, Stephen B., and Katalina Tahaafe-Williams, eds. *Contextual Theology for the Twenty-first Century.* Cambridge: James Clarke, 2011.

Bidwell, Kevin J. *"The Church as the Image of the Trinity": A Critical Evaluation of Miroslav Volf's Ecclesial Model.* Eugene: Wipf and Stock, 2011.

Bieler, Andrea, and Luise Schottroff. *The Eucharist: Bodies, Bread, and Resurrection.* Minneapolis: Fortress, 2007.

Boersma, Hans. *Heavenly Participation: The Weaving of a Sacramental Tapestry.* Grand Rapids: Eerdmans, 2011.

Boeve, Lieven. "Thinking Sacramental Presence in a Postmodern Context: A Playground for Theological Renew." In *Sacramental Presence in a Postmodern Context*, edited by Lieven Boeve and L. Leijssen, 3–35. Leuven: Leuven University Press, 2001.

Bordeianu, Radu. "Orthodox-Catholic Dialogue: Retrieving Eucharistic Ecclesiology." *Journal of Ecumenical Studies* 44 (2009) 239–65.

Borne, Etinne. *Modern Atheism*. London: Burs & Oates, 1961.

Bourdieu, Pierre. *Outline of a Theory of Practice*. Translated by Richard Nice. New York: Cambridge University Press, 1977.

———. "Structures, Habitus, Practice." In *The Logic of Practice*, translated by Richard Nice, 52–65. Cambridge: Polity, 1990.

Bradshaw, Paul F. "Ancient Church Orders: A Continuing Enigma." In *The Search for the Origins of Christian Worship: Sources and Methods for the Study of Early Liturgy*, 80–110. London: SPCK, 2002.

———. *Early Christian Worship: A Basic Introduction to Ideas and Practice*. Collegeville: Liturgical, 1996.

———, ed. *Essays on Early Eastern Eucharistic Prayers*. Collegeville: Liturgical, 1997.

———. *Eucharistic Origins*. London: SPCK, 2004.

———. *Reconstructing Early Christian Worship*. London: SPCK, 2009.

———. *The Search for the Origins of Christian Worship: Sources and Methods for the Study of Early Liturgy*. London: SPCK, 2002.

Bradshaw, Paul F., and Bryan Spinks, eds. *Liturgy in Dialogue: Essays in Memory of Ronald Jasper*. Collegeville: Liturgical, 1993.

Brown, Delwin, et al., eds. *Converging on Culture: Theologians in Dialogue with Cultural Analysis and Criticism*. Oxford: Oxford University Press, 2001.

Brueggemann, Walter. *The Covenanted Self: Explorations in Law and Covenant*. Minneapolis: Fortress, 1999.

Buckley, Michael J. *Denying and Disclosing God: The Ambiguous Progress of Modern Atheism*. New Haven: Yale University Press, 2004.

Chappel, James. "The Catholic Origins of Totalitarianism Theory in Interwar Europe." *Modern Intellectual History* 8 (2011) 561–90.

Chauvet, Louis-Marie. "The Broken Bread as Theological Figure of Eucharistic Presence." In *Sacramental Presence in a Postmodern Context*, edited by Lieven Boeve and L. Leijssen, 236–62. Leuven: Leuven University Press, 2001.

Chibuko, Patrick Chukwudezie. "Forestation—Deforestation—Reforestation: Implications for Ecology and Liturgy in Dialogue." *AFER* 52 (2010) 189–212.

Chupungco, Anscar J. *Liturgical Incultration: Sacramentals, Religiosity, and Catechesis*. Collegeville: Liturgical, 1992.

Cobb, Kelton. *The Blackwell Guide to Theology and Popular Culture*. Malden: Blackwell, 2005.

Collins, Paul M. *Trinitarian Theology West and East: Karl Barth, the Cappadocian Fathers, and John Zizioulas*. Oxford: Oxford University Press, 2001.

De Lubac, Henri. *Augustianism and Modern Theology*. Translated by Lancelot Sheppard. London: Chapman, 1969.

———. *A Brief Catechesis on Nature and Grace*. Translated by Richard Arnandez. San Francisco: Ignatius, 1984.

———. *Catholicism: A Study of the Corporate Destiny of Mankind*. Translated by Lancelot C. Sheppard. New York: The New American Library, 1964.

———. *The Christian Faith: An Essay on the Structure of the Apostles' Creed.* Translated by Illtyd Treth. San Francisco: Ignatius, 1986.

———. *The Church: Paradox and Mystery.* Translated by James R. Dunne. Shannon: Ecclesia, 1969.

———. *Corpus Mysticum: The Eucharist and the Church in the Middle Ages.* Translated by Gemma Simmonds. Edited by Laurence Paul Hemming and Susan Frank Parsons. London: SCM, 2006.

———. *The Discovery of God.* Translated by Alexander Dru. Edinburgh: T. & T. Clark, 1996.

———. *The Drama of Atheist Humanism.* Translated by Edith M. Riley. Cleveland: World, 1950.

———. *The Four Senses of Scripture.* Vol. 1 of *Medieval Exegesis.* Translated by Mark Sebanc. Grand Rapids: Eerdmans, 1998.

———. *History and Spirit: The Understanding of Scripture according to Origen.* Translated by Anne Englund Nash and Juvenal Merriell. San Francisco: Ignatius, 2007.

———. *The Motherhood of the Church.* Translated by Sergia Englund. San Francisco: Ignatius Press, 1982.

———. *The Mystery of the Supernatural.* Translated by Rosemary Sheed. New York: Crossroad Publishing Company, 1998.

———. *The Religion of Teilhard de Chardin.* Translated by Rène Hague. New York: Desclee, 1967.

———. *At the Service of the Church: Henri de Lubac Reflects on the Circumstances that Occasioned His Writings.* Translated by Anne Englund Nash. San Francisco: Ignatius, 1993.

———. *The Splendor of the Church.* Translated by Michael Mason. San Francisco: Ignatius, 1956.

———. *Surnaturel.* Paris: Aubier, 1946.

———. *Theology in History.* Translated by Anne Englund Nash. San Francisco: Ignatius, 1996.

Del Colle, Ralph. "Communion and the Trinity: The Free Church Ecclesiology of Miroslav Volf—a Catholic Response." *Pneuma* 22 (2000) 303–27.

Denysenko, Nicholas E. "Primacy, Synodality, and Collegiality in Orthodoxy: A Liturgical Model." *Journal of Ecumenical Studies* 48 (2013) 20–44.

Dix, Gregory. *The Shape of the Liturgy.* London: Continuum, 2005.

Doyle, Dennis M. *Communion Ecclesiology: Vision and Versions.* Maryknoll: Orbis, 2001.

———. "Henri de Lubac and the Roots of Communion Ecclesiology." *Theological Studies* 60 (1999) 209–27.

Dulles, Avery. Review of *After Our Likeness: The Church as the Image of the Trinity,* by Miroslav Volf. *First Things* 87 (1998) 50–52.

Durheim, Benjamin. "The Possibility of Eucharistic Sharing: An Application of John Zizioulas's Theology." *Worship* 85 (2011) 290–305.

Durkheim, Emile *The Elementary Forms of Religious Life.* Translated by Karen E. Fields. New York: Free, 1995.

Edwall, Pehr, eds. *Ways of Worship: The Report of a Theological Commission of Faith and Order.* London: SCM, 1951.

Edwards, Denis. "Eucharist and Ecology: Keeping Memorial of Creation." *Worship* 82 (2008) 194–213.

Erickson, John, and Paul Laraz, eds. *The Paschal Service*. Wayne: Orthodox Christian, 1990.

Fiddes, Paul S. "Ecclesiology and Ethnography: Two Disciplines, Two Worlds?" In *Perspectives on Ecclesiology and Ethnography*, edited by Pete Ward, 13–35. Grand Rapids: Eerdmans, 2012.

Ford, David F. *Self and Salvation: Being Transformed*. Cambridge: Cambridge University Press, 1999.

Fox, Patricia A. *God as Communion: John Zizioulas, Elizabeth Johnson, and the Retrieval of the Symbol of the Triune God*. Collegeville: Liturgical, 2001.

Freeman, Curtis. "Where Two or Three are Gathered: Communion Ecclesiology in the Free Church." *Perspectives in Religious Studies* 31 (2004) 259–72.

Geertz, Clifford. "Ethos, World-view and the Analysis of Sacred Symbols." *Anticho Review* 17 (1957) 421–37.

Gorringe, T. J. "Liberation Theology and Cultural Politics." In *Furthering Humanity: A Theology of Culture*, 149–73. Burlington: Ashgate, 2004.

Grumett, David. *De Lubac: A Guide for the Perplexed*. London: T. & T. Clark, 2007.

———. "The Eucharistic Cosmology of Teilhard de Chardin." *Theology* 110 (2007) 22–30.

———. "Eucharist, Matter and the Supernatural: Why de Lubac Needs Teilhard." *International Journal of Systematic Theology* 10 (2008) 165–78.

Gunton, Colin E. *The One, The Three, and The Many: God, Creation and the Culture of Modernity*. Cambridge: Cambridge University Press, 1993.

Halloran, Nathan. "The Flesh of the Church: De Lubac, Marion, and the Site of the Phenomenality of Givenness." *Irish Theological Quarterly* 75 (2010) 29–44.

Harrison, Nonna Verna. "Zizioulas on Communion and Otherness." *St. Vladimir's Seminary Quarterly* 43 (1998) 273–300.

Hessel-Robinson, et al., eds. *Spirit and Nature: The Study of Christian Spirituality in a Time of Ecological Urgency*. Eugene: Pickwick, 2011.

Hollon, Bryan C. *Everything is Sacred: Spiritual Exegesis in the Political Theology of Henri de Lubac*. Eugene: Cascade, 2009.

Hopkins, Dwight N., and Sheila Greeve Davaney, eds. *Changing Conversations: Religious Reflection and Cultural Analysis*. New York: Routledge, 1996.

Hopper, Paul. *Rebuilding Communities in an Age of Individualism*. Aldershot: Ashgate, 2003.

Hughes, Kevin L. "The 'Fourfold Sense': De Lubac, Blondel and Contemporary Theology." *The Heythrop Journal* 4 (2001) 451–46.

Irwin, Kevin W. *Context and Text: Method in Liturgical Theology*. Collegeville: Liturgical, 1994.

Jacques, Geneviève. "Confronting the Challenge of Exclusion." *Ecumenical Review* 46 (1994) 328–33.

Johnson, Mark. *The Body in the Mind: The Bodily Basis of Meaning, Imagination, and Reason*. Chicago: University of Chicago Press, 1987.

———. *The Meaning of the Body: Aesthetics of Human Understanding*. Chicago: University of Chicago Press, 2007.

———, ed. *Philosophical Perspectives on Metaphor*. Minneapolis: University of Minnesota Press, 1981.

Jones, Christopher. "Loosing and Binding: The Liturgical Mediation of Forgiveness." In *Forgiveness and Truth*, edited by Alistair McFadyen and Marcel Sarot, 31–52. New York: T. & T. Clark, 2001.

Jones, L. Gregory. *Embodying Forgiveness: A Theological Analysis.* Grand Rapids: Eerdmans, 1995.

Junker, Tércio Bretanha. "The Prophetic Dimension of Liturgy: Transformation." PhD diss., Garrett-Evangelical Theological Seminary, 2003.

Kearney, Richard. "Ethics and the Postmodern Imagination." *Thought* 62 (1987) 39–58.

Keightley, Georgia Masters. "The Church's Laity: Called to be Creation's Priests." *Worship* 84 (2010) 309–27.

Kellenher, Margaret Mary. "Liturgy, Culture, and the Challenge of Catholicity." *Worship* 84 (2010) 98–120.

Khalil, Issa J. "Ecological Crisis: An Eastern Christian Perspective." *St. Vladimir's Theological Quarterly* 22 (1978) 193–211.

Klinghardt, Matthias. "A Typology of the Communal Meal." In *Meals in the Early Christian World: Social Formation, Experimentation, and Conflict at the Table,* edited by Dennis E. Smith and Hal E. Taussig, 9–22. New York: Palgrave Macmillan, 2012.

Knight, Douglas H. *The Theology of John Zizioulas: Personhood and the Church.* Aldershot: Ashgate, 2007.

Komonchak, Joseph A. "Theology and Culture at Mid-Century: The Example of Henri de Lubac." *Theological Studies* 51 (1990) 579–602.

Lai, Pan-chiu. "Cultural Studies and Theology in Tillichian Perspective: With Special Reference to Sino-Theology." *Sino-Christian Studies* (2010) 55–87.

Lakoff, George, and Mark Johnson. *Metaphors We Live By.* Chicago: University of Chicago Press, 1980.

Lathrop, Gordon W. "The Cardinal Directions: Liturgical Reorientation." In *Holy Ground: A Liturgical Cosmology,* 51–67. Minneapolis: Fortress, 2003.

———. "Eucharist and Earth-Care." In *Holy Ground: A Liturgical Cosmology,* 125–52. Minneapolis: Fortress, 2003.

———. *Holy People: A Liturgical Ecclesiology.* Minneapolis: Fortress, 2006.

———. *Holy Things: A Liturgical Theology.* Minneapolis: Fortress, 1993.

Lee, Man-yiu. *The Church as Person in the Theologies of Dietrich Bonhoeffer, John D. Zizioulas and Jürgen Moltmann.* Hong Kong: Nation-Blessings Consultancy Company, 2013.

Loudovikos, Nicholaos. "Christian Life and Institutional Church." In *The Theology of John Zizioulas: Personhood and the Church,* edited by Douglas Knight, 125–45. Aldershot: Ashgate, 2007.

———. *A Eucharistic Ontology: Maximus the Confessor's Eschatological Ontology of Being as Dialogical Reciprocity.* Translated by Elizabeth Theokritoff. Brookline: Holy Cross Orthodox, 2010.

———. "Person instead of Grace and Dictated Otherness: John Zizioulas' Final Theological Position." *The Heythrop Journal* 52 (2011) 684–99.

Louth, Andrew. *Maximus the Confessor.* London: Routledge, 1996.

Lozano, Alix "Living out of Hope from a Place of Exclusion: Service Rooted in Solidarity." *Conrad Grebel Review* 19 (2001) 33–40.

Manning, Russell Re. *Theology at the End of Culture: Paul Tillich's Theology of Culture and Art.* Leuven: Peeters, 2005.

Mayeski, Marie Anne. "Reading the Word in a Eucharistic Context: The Shape and Methods of Early Medieval Exegesis." In *Medieval Liturgy: A Book of Essays,* edited by Lizette Larson-Miller, 61–84. New York: Garland, 1997.

McFadyen, Alistair, and Marcel Sarot, eds. *Forgiveness and Truth: Explorations in Contemporary Theology*. New York: T. & T. Clark, 2001.

McPartlan, Paul. *The Eucharist Makes the Church: Henri de Lubac and John Zizioulas in Dialogue*. Edinburgh: T. & T. Clark, 1993.

Meeks, Wayne A. *The Origins of Christian Morality: The First Two Centuries*. New Haven: Yale University Press, 1993.

Merleau-Ponty, Maurice. *Phenomenology of Perception*. Translated by Colin Smith. London: Routledge & K. Paul, 1962.

———. *The Structure of Behavior*. Translated by Alden L. Fisher. Boston: Beacon, 1967.

Metz, Johannes Baptist. *Faith in History and Society: Toward a Practical Fundamental Theology*. Translated by David Smith. New York: Seabury, 1980.

Meyendorff, John. *Christ in the Eastern Christian Thought*. Crestwood: St. Vladimir's Seminary, 1975.

Milbank, John. *The Suspended Middle: Henri de Lubac and the Debate Concerning the Supernatural*. Grand Rapids: Eerdmans, 2005.

Mitchell, Nathan D. "Contextualizing Henri de Lubac's Work." *Worship* 84 (2010) 275–84.

———. "*ECCLESIAE DEI SOCIARI; ECCLESIAE INCOPORARI; IN CORPUS ECCLESIAE TRANSIRE*," *Worship* 84 (2010) 345–54.

Moltmann, Jürgen. *The Church in the Power of the Spirit: A Contribution to Messianic Ecclesiology*. Minneapolis: Fortress, 1993.

———. *The Trinity and the Kingdom: The Doctrine of God*. New York: Harper & Row, 1981.

Morgan, Janine Paden. "Emerging Eucharist: Formative Ritualizing in British Emerging Churches." PhD diss., Fuller Theological Seminary, School of Theology, 2009.

Murken, Todd B. *Take and Eat, and Take the Consequences: How Receiving the Lord's Supper is an Action that Makes a Difference*. New York: Peter Lang, 2002.

Nicholas, Richard A. *The Eucharist as the Center of Theology: A Comparative Study*. New York: Peter Lang, 2005.

Niebuhr, H. Richard. *Christ and Culture*. New York: HarperCollins, 1951.

Papanikolaou, Aristotle. *Being with God: Trinity, Apophaticism, and Divine-Human Communion*: Notre Dame: University of Notre Dame Press, 2006.

Pecklers, Keith F. *Worship*. London: Continuum, 2003.

Pecknold, C. C. "Migrations of the Host: Fugitive Democracy and the *Corpus Mysticum*." *Political Theology* 11 (2010) 77–101.

Pivarnik, R. Gabriel. *Toward a Trinitarian Theology of Liturgical Participation*. Collegeville: Liturgical, 2012.

Plantinga, Cornelius. *Not the Way It's Supposed to Be: A Breviary of Sin*. Grand Rapids: Eerdmans, 1995.

Ray, Walter D. "The Strasbourg Papyrus." In *Essays on Early Eastern Eucharistic Prayers*, edited by Paul E. Bradshaw, 39–56. Collegeville: Liturgical, 1997.

Reimer, A. James. "Miroslav Volf: One of the New Theologians." *Conrad Grebel Review* 18 (2000) 3–19.

Rubin, Miri. *Corpus Christi: The Eucharist in Late Medieval Culture*. New York: Cambridge University Press, 1991.

Russell, Edward. "Reconsidering Relational Anthropology: A Critical Assessment of John Zizioulas's Theological Anthropology." *International Journal of Systematic Theology* 5 (2003) 168–86.

Sahin, Bican, and Nezahat Altuntas. "Between Enlightened Exclusion and Conscientious Inclusion: Tolerating the Muslims in Germany." *Journal of Muslim Minority Affairs* 29 (2009) 27–41.

Saliers, Donald E. "Liturgy and Ethics: Some New Beginnings." In *Introduction to Christian Ethics: A Reader*, edited by Ronald P. Hamel and Kenneth B. Himes, 175–86. New York: Paulist, 1989.

Santmire, H. Paul. *Ritualizing Nature: Renewing Christian Liturgy in a Time of Crisis*. Minneapolis: Fortress, 2008.

Scharen, Christian. "Ecclesiology 'From the Body': Ethnographic Notes toward a Carnal Theology." In *Perspectives on Ecclesiology and Ethnography*, edited by Pete Ward, 50–70. Grand Rapids: Eerdmans, 2012.

Scott, Margaret. *The Eucharist and Social Justice*. New York: Paulist, 2009.

Sheldrake, Philip. *Spaces for the Sacred: Place, Memory, and Identity*. Baltimore: The Johns Hopkins University Press, 2001.

Shepherd, Andrew. "The 'Other', the 'Gift', and 'Priesthood': Zizioulas' Eucharistic and Eschatological Theology of Creation." *Stimulus* 15 (2007) 3–8.

Shriver, Donald W. *An Ethic for Enemies: Forgiveness in Politics*. New York: Oxford University Press, 1995.

Smith, Dennis E. *From Symposium to Eucharist: The Banquet in the Early Christian World*. Minneapolis: Fortress, 2003.

Smith, Dennis E., and Hal E. Taussig. *Many Tables: The Eucharist in the New Testament and Liturgy Today*. London: SCM, 1990.

———, eds. *Meals in the Early Christian World: Social Formation, Experimentation, and Conflict at the Table*. New York: Palgrave Macmillan, 2012.

Smith, James K. A. *Desiring the Kingdom: Worship, Worldview, and Cultural Formation*. Grand Rapids: Baker Academic, 2009.

———. *Imagining the Kingdom: How Worship Works*. Grand Rapids: Baker Academic, 2013.

Smith, Jonathan Z. "The Influence of Symbols upon Social Change: A Place on which to Stand." *Worship* 44 (1979) 457–74.

———. *To Take Place: Toward Theory in Ritual*. Chicago: University of Chicago Press, 1987.

Sours, Stephen Bentley. "Eucharist and Anthropology: Seeking Convergence on Eucharistic Sacrifice between Catholics and Methodists." PhD diss., Duke University, 2011.

Spijker, Ineke van't, ed. *The Multiple Meaning of Scripture: The Role of Exegesis in Early-Christian and Medieval Culture*. Boston: Brill, 2009.

Spinks, Bryan D. *Do This in Remembrance of Me: The Eucharist from the Early Church to the Present Day*. London: SCM, 2013.

Stoker, Wessel, and W. L. van der Merwe, eds. *Culture and Transcendence: A Typology of Transcendence*. Leuven: Walpole, 2012.

Stringer, Martin D. *A Sociological History of Christian Worship*. Cambridge: Cambridge University Press, 2005.

Swinton, John. "'Where is Your Church?'" Moving toward a Hospitable and Sanctified Ethnography." In *Perspectives on Ecclesiology and Ethnography*, edited by Pete Ward, 71–92. Grand Rapids: Eerdmans, 2012.

Tanner, Kathryn. *Theories of Culture: A New Agenda for Theology*. Minneapolis: Fortress, 1997.

Taussig, Hal. *In the Beginning was the Meal: Social Experimentation and Early Christian Identity*. Minneapolis: Fortress, 2009.

———. "The Hellenistic and Early Christian Social Practice of Festive Meals." In *In the Beginning was the Meal: Social Experimentation and Early Christian Identity*, 21–54. Minneapolis: Fortress, 2009.

———. "Ritual Analysis: A New Method for the study of Early Christian Meals." In *In the Beginning was the Meal: Social Experimentation and Early Christian Identity*, 55–85. Minneapolis: Fortress, 2009

Thunberg, Lars. *Man and the Cosmos: The Vision of St. Maximus the Confessor*. Crestwood: St. Vladimir's Seminary, 1985.

Tillich, Paul. *Theology of Culture*. Edited by Robert C. Kimball. New York: Oxford University Press, 1959.

Torrance, Alan J. *Persons in Communion: An Essay on Trinitarian Description and Human Participation*. Edinburgh: T. & T. Clark, 1996.

Veliyannoor, Paulson Varkey. "Transformation in 'E': The Structure and Dynamics of the Lived Experience of the Eucharist." PhD diss., Pacifica Graduate Institute, 2011.

Vincie, Catherine. *Celebrating the Divine Mystery: A Primer in Liturgical Theology*. Collegeville: Liturgical, 2009.

Volf, Miroslav. "'After the Grave in the Air': True Reconciliation through Unconditional Embrace." *Journal of European Baptist Studies* 2 (2002) 5–11.

———. *After Our Likeness: The Church as the Image of the Trinity*. Grand Rapids: Eerdmans, 1998.

———. "Being as God is: Trinity and Generosity." In *God's Life in Trinity*, edited by Miroslav Volf and Michael Welker, 3–12. Minneapolis: Fortress, 2006.

———. *The End of Memory: Remembering Rightly in a Violent World*. Grand Rapids: Eerdmans, 2006.

———. *Exclusion and Embrace: A Theological Exploration of Identity, Otherness, and Reconciliation*. Nashville: Abingdon, 1996.

———. "Exclusion and Embrace: Theological Reflections in the Wake of 'Ethnic Cleansing.'" *Communio Viatorum* 35 (1993) 263–87.

———. "The Final Reconciliation: Reflections on a Social Dimension of the Eschatological Transition." *Modern Theology* 16 (2000) 91–113.

———. *Flourishing: Why We Need Religion in a Globalized Word*. New Haven: Yale University Press, 2015.

———. "Forgiveness, Reconciliation, and Justice: A Theological Contribution to a More Peaceful Social Environment." *Journal of International Studies* 29 (2000) 861–77.

———. *Free of Charge: Giving and Forgiving in a Culture Stripped of Grace*. Grand Rapids: Zondervan, 2005.

———. "God's Forgiveness and Ours: Memory of Interrogations, Interrogation of Memory." *Anglican Theological Review* 89 (2007) 213–25.

———. "Liberation Theology after the End of History." *Modern Theology* 19 (2003) 261–69.

———. "Living with the 'Other.'" *Journal of Ecumenical Studies* 39 (2002) 8–25.

———. "Memory, Eschatology, Eucharist." *Liturgy* 22 (2007) 27–38.

———. *A Public Faith: How Followers of Christ Should Serve the Common Good*. Grand Rapids: Brazos, 2011.

———. "The Social Meaning of Reconciliation." *Interpretation* 54 (2000) 158–72.

———. "Soft Difference: Theological Reflections on the Relation between Church and Culture in 1 Peter." *Ex auditu* 10 (1994) 15–30.

———. "Theology for a Way of Life." *Ex auditu* 17 (2001) 125–41.

———. "The Trinity is Our Social Program": The Doctrine of the Trinity and the Shape of Social Engagement." *Modern Theology* 14 (1998) 403–23.

———. "A Vision of Embrace: Theological Perspective on Cultural Identity and Conflict." *Ecumenical Review* 47 (1995) 195–205.

Vosloo, Robert. "Reconciliation as the Embodiment of Memory and Hope." *Journal of Theology for South Africa* 109 (2001) 25–40.

Wallenfang, Donlad L. "Sacramental Givenness: The Notion of Givenness in Husserl, Heidegger, and Marion, and Its Import for Interpreting the Phenomenality of the Eucharist." *Philosophy & Theology* 22 (2012) 131–54.

Wandel, Lee Palmer. *The Eucharist in the Reformation: Incarnation and Liturgy.* New York: Cambridge University Press, 2006.

Ward, Graham. *Cultural Transformation and Religious Practice.* Cambridge: Cambridge University Press, 2005.

Ward, Pete, ed. *Perspectives on Ecclesiology and Ethnography.* Grand Rapids: Eerdmans, 2012.

Welker, Michael. *Schöpfung und Wirklichkeit.* Neukirchen-Vluyn: Neukirchener Verlag, 1995.

Witvliet, John D. *Worship Seeking Understanding: Windows into Christian Practice.* Grand Rapids: Baker Academic, 2003.

Wolterstorff, Nicholas. *Hearing the Call: Liturgy, Justice, Church and Word.* Edited by Mark R. Gornik and Gregory Thompson. Grand Rapids: Eerdmans, 2011.

———. "Justice as a Condition of Authentic Liturgy." *Theology Today* 48 (1991) 6–21.

Wood, Susan K. "Henri de Lubac, SJ (1896–1991) Theologian of the Church." *Theology Today* 62 (2005) 318–28.

———. *Spiritual Exegesis and the Church in the Theology of Henri de Lubac.* Grand Rapids: Eerdmans, 1998.

World Council of Churches. *Baptism, Eucharist, and Ministry*, Faith and Order Paper Series, no. III. Geneva: World Council of Churches, 1982.

Zizioulas, John. *Being as Communion: Studies in Personhood and the Church.* Crestwood: St. Vladimir's Seminary, 1985.

———. *Communion and Otherness.* Edited by Paul McPartlan. London: T. & T. Clark, 2006.

———. "Ecological Asceticism: A Cultural Revolution." *Sourozh* 67 (1997) 22–25.

———. *Eucharist, Bishop, the Church: The Unity of the Church in the Divine Eucharist and the Bishop during the First Three Centuries.* Brookline: Holy Cross Orthodox, 2001.

———. *The Eucharistic Communion and the World.* Edited by Luke Ben Tallon. London: T. & T. Clark, 2011.

———. "Eucharistic Prayer and Life." *Emmanuel* 81 (1975) 462–70.

———. *Lectures in Christian Dogmatics.* Edited by Douglas H. Knight. London: T. & T. Clark, 2006.

———. "The Mystery of the Church in the Orthodox Tradition." *One in Christ* 24 (1988) 294–303.

———. *The One and the Many: Studies on God, Man, the Church, and the World Today.* Edited by Gregory Edwards. Alhambra: Sebastian, 2010.

———. "Preserving God's Creation: Three lectures on Theology and Ecology—Lecture Three." *King's Theological Review* 13 (1990) 1–5.

———. "Primitive Christianity: The Original Spirituality." *Church* 3 (1987) 10–14.

———. "The Theological Problem of Reception." *One in Christ* 21 (1985) 187–93.

Index

abusive culture on creation, countering, 62

academic publications, of Zizioulas, 109

actualization, of truly personal existence, 55

Afanassieff, Nicholas, 52

affirmation of justice, granting of forgiveness and, 98

After His Likeness (Volf), 75, 76, 85, 117, 139, 140

agency, 91, 113

agents, resisting cultural currents, 133

aggressors, facilitating, 97

alienation, theological responses to, 11

aliens, Christians recognizing themselves as, 89

all otherness, fear of, 61

alter christus, 52, 123

"alternative cultural formation," Christian worship as, 15

anaphora

of the "Apostolic Constitutions," 128

to the Creator God as Eucharist, 62

receiving and lifting up of gifts known as, 53

reflecting the unreserved acceptance of creation, 63

subscription to the patristic teachings of, 140

anaphora (lifting up and giving back) prayer, of St. Basil and St. John Chrysostom, 63

ancient Church, faithful brought with them gifts of creation, 129

Anglican-Orthodox dialogue, co-chairman of, 109

"apophatic icon," Eucharist as, 73

apophatic theology, going beyond the economic Trinity, 49

Aquinas, Thomas

de Lubac's understanding of, 26

on Grace, 119

on nature, 26

thought on the Eucharist, 12

Arbuckle, Gerald A., 10–11

arche (causality), 55, 116

Armenian liturgy, ancient, 128

asymmetric hierarchy, caused by *monarchia*, 58

asymmetric structure, of the church and the Eucharist, 57

asymmetric trinitarian existence, 134

asymmetrical doctrine of the Trinity, 118

asymmetrical structure of the Trinity, 72

asymmetrical trinitarian communion, 121

asymmetry, in the Trinity, 58, 70

Athanasius, 124n35

atheism, 35–36

Augustine, 38, 39–40, 128

"Augustinian anthropology," 15

awareness, of cultural currents, 108–10

baptism

constitutive of the church, 84

incorporation in, 38, 58, 95

Catholicism (de Lubac), 43
catholicity
  of Christians, 80
  of the divine persons, 79
  of the Eucharist, 51
  at the inter-ecclesial level, 80
causality (*arche*), 55, 116
*Changing Conversations: Religious
  Reflection and Cultural Analysis*
  (Hopkins and Davaney), 10
charismata, Christians receiving, 84
charity, as individual obligation, 35
Chauvet, Louis-Marie, 11, 68
cheap forgiveness, 97
Christ
  as a corporate personality, 51
  gave his life sacrificially to all others,
    67
  hypostasization in, 55, 65, 137
  indwelling the church, 80
  power of the priesthood given and
    defined by, 45
  as priest of creation, 121
  priest receiving power conferred
    by, 40
  promising to protect the identities of
    victims, 94
  real presence of in the Eucharist, 29
  revealed in the Eucharist, 53
  self-giving of, 96
"Christ against Culture" type, 3
Christ and Culture (Niebuhr), 2
"Christ the Transformer of Culture"
  type, 3
"Christian dignity," 40
Christian discourses, relation with
  cultural transformation, 10
Christian ethnic and cultural identity,
  otherness part and parcel of, 88
Christian identity, receiving further
  attention, 4
Christian liturgy. *See* liturgy
Christian meal groups, meant to be
  countercultural, 5
Christian Mystery, Eucharist lost its
  place in, 29
Christian mysticism of unity, as trini-
  tarian, 30

Christian symbols, scholarships of, 11
Christianity, causing conflicts leading
  to social exclusion, 87–88
Christians
  adopting a meek attitude, 89
  distancing themselves from their
    own culture, 88
  participating in the Eucharist, 102
  pre-occupied with concerns belong-
    ing to private realms, 35
  receiving spiritual sustenance
    through the Eucharist, 85
christocentric model, of de Lubac, 31
christological hypostasization, extended to humanity, 56
Christology and Pneumatology, synthesis of, 50
Chupungco, Anscar J., 9
church
  as charismatic and polycentric-
    participative, 84
  constituting the Eucharist while be-
    ing constituted by it, 52
  corresponding to and reflecting the
    Trinity, 78
  countering hierarchical and totali-
    tarian cultural currents, 131
  as a cultural minority within the
    larger society, 3–4
  dialogue with Greek culture in early
    church history, 68
  embracing the divine, 27
  entering into conversation with the
    prevailing culture in depth, 68
  four-layer structure of, 123
  freeing individuals from restrictions
    of power, 41
  growing institutional power of, 123
  heavily imbued with institutional
    power, 36
  hierarchy, 31, 41
  impacted by individualism, 35
  as *koinonia* (communion of God), 50
  mutuality of members, 76
  producing the Eucharist, 31–32
  recapitulating all creation to God
    through the Eucharist, 53

church *(continued)*
  reduced to a social body like a mere congregation, 29
  relating to power in a multicultural world, 11
  structures, 84
  temptation to become totalitarian, 36
  traditions of the three theologians, 138
  uniting the world and referring it back to God, 64
  urging to be self-critical to its tendency to being over-hierarchical, 45
  as a visible communion of saints bounded by covenant, 82
church model, of "polycentric and symmetrical reciprocity of the many," 76
churches
  all are catholic, 91
  cannot be internal to one another, 80
  guiding the faithful to engage, 113
circular love in the Trinity, movement to the cross, 94
"circumincession," of the persons of the Trinity, 44
clerical totalitarianism, 36, 45
Cobb, Kelton, 10
cognitive specification, of confession, 83
coincident unity-of-identity, 44, 140
collectivism, reaction against leading to individualism, 111–12
commensurability and incommensurability, between Christian and non-Christian value systems, 89
communal meals, as the center of activities of early Christian communities, 4
communion
  constitutive of otherness, 56
  in the Eucharist, 65
  as "freedom for the other," 111
  generating otherness and not threatening it, 65
  of God's people, 50

including all creation, 64
of otherness, 111, 137
prophetic and critical element in, 68
in the Trinity not egalitarian but asymmetric, 57
"communitarian spirit," 38
"community-forming ritual," 14
complementarity
  in a cross-church tradition study, 139–40
  of ecclesial and eucharistic realism, 41
  of "the Eucharist makes the Church" and "the Church produces the Eucharist," 122
  of eucharistic realism and ecclesial realism, 31–32
complementary relationship, of the divine persons, 78–79
complementary use, of Zizioulas's idea of otherness, 140
completion, theological details of, 44–45
"completion-by-means-of-each-other," 140
"concorporation," concept of, 38
confession, 83
Converging on Culture: Theologians in Dialogue with Cultural Analysis and Criticism, 10
corpus mysticum, 29
corpus verum (true body), 29
correspondences, between the Trinity and the church, 77
cosmic dimension, of the Eucharist, 53
cosmic significance, of Jesus' crucifixion, 5
cosmological dimension, of the Eucharist, 54
cosmological intention, of the Eucharist, 33–34
cosmological interpretation, of the Eucharist, 74
cosmology, connecting the Eucharist to, 59
cosmos, created *ex nihilo* by God, 63–64
Council of Trent, teachings of, 128

ecclesial communities, inviting to
critique themselves, 113
ecclesial existence, different from the
lifestyle of the larger society, 90
ecclesial fatherhood, reflecting Trinitarian Fatherhood, 58
ecclesial hypostasization, transforming
the catholic mode of existence
by, 112
ecclesial or catholic person, Volf adopting Zizioulas's idea of, 102
ecclesial realism
of the Eucharist, 111
re-directing attention to, 31
relationship with eucharistic realism,
32, 122
"ecclesial socialization," in the congregation, 80
ecclesial unity, sacrament of the Eucharist as an instrument of, 37
ecclesiality, of the church, 81–85
ecclesiastical life, impact of individualism on today's, 61
ecclesiastical polity, not always influenced by theologians' discourses,
123
ecclesiological (in the order of communion), 116
ecclesiological aspect
de Lubac focusing on, 138
in the order of communion, 122–26
"ecclesiological monophysitism," 36
ecclesiology
based on trinitarian theology for
Zizioulas, 50
ethnographical studies on, 21
making the trinitarian doctrine
relevant, 49
trinitarian doctrine decisive for, 48
of Volf as not characteristically
eucharistic, 85, 135
ecological activism, ethos stopping, 69
ecological crisis
as a cultural issue, 62
as global and cultural, 109
as a global concern, 60
shaping ecclesial communities to
address, 14

ecological problem, as a "crisis of culture," 59–60
economic Trinity
not exhausting the immanent Trinity, 49
ordering, 59
Volf focusing on, 77
ecumenical dialogue, 1, 75
ecumenical recognition, of the Eucharist, 101
Edwards, Denis, 63
egalitarian church model, 81, 85
egalitarian communion, of the church,
125
egalitarian doctrine, of the Trinity for
the Free Church, 76
egalitarian ecclesial model, facilitating
the formation of catholic agents,
138
ek-stasis, 56–57
elite, European culture of, 86
embrace
connecting to the Eucharist, 101
Eucharist as the sacrament of, 135
as space for others, 92–95
"Emerging Eucharist: Formative
Ritualizing in British Emerging
Churches" (Morgan), 12–13
environmental issues, effectively addressing, 70
epiclesis, 27, 64
episcopacy, centrality in the ecclesiology, 59
episcopal presidency of the Eucharist,
central to Zizioulas's ecclesiology,
51
episcopal-centric church model, shaping, 122
episcopal-centric structure, of the Eucharist application to the church,
59
equality, among individual members as
well as churches, 81
eros, of the Father extended to human
beings, 65
eschatological fulfillment, of the perfect
communion of believers, 81

43408360R00108

Made in the USA
Middletown, DE
09 May 2017